MESSI
vs
RONALDO

Matt
Haines

MESSI

VS

RONALDO

2018 Edition

LUCA CAIOLI

ICON

Published in the UK and USA in 2017 by
Icon Books Ltd, Omnibus Business Centre,
39–41 North Road, London N7 9DP
email: info@iconbooks.com
www.iconbooks.com

Sold in the UK, Europe and Asia
by Faber & Faber Ltd, Bloomsbury House,
74–77 Great Russell Street, London WC1B 3DA or their agents

Distributed in the UK, Europe and Asia
by Grantham Book Services,
Trent Road, Grantham NG31 7XQ

Distributed in Australia and New Zealand
by Allen & Unwin Pty Ltd,
PO Box 8500, 83 Alexander Street,
Crows Nest, NSW 2065

Distributed in South Africa
by Jonathan Ball, Office B4, The District,
41 Sir Lowry Road, Woodstock 7925

Distributed in India by Penguin Books India,
7th Floor, Infinity Tower – C, DLF Cyber City,
Gurgaon 122002, Haryana

Distributed in Canada by Publishers Group Canada,
76 Stafford Street, Unit 300, Toronto, Ontario M6J 2S1

Distributed in the USA
by Publishers Group West,
1700 Fourth Street, Berkeley, CA 94710

ISBN: 978-1-78578-277-0

Typeset in New Baskerville by Marie Doherty

Printed and bound in the UK by Clays Ltd, St Ives plc

About the author

Luca Caioli is the bestselling author of *Messi, Ronaldo* and *Neymar*. A renowned Italian sports journalist, he lives in Spain.

Contents

1   Messi and Cristiano, Cristiano and Messi   1

2   The Rosarino versus the Madeiran   7

3   30–22   15

4   Argentina versus Portugal   57

5   Duels   75

6   Goals   91

7   5–4   103

8   Playing style   117

9   The delivery boy versus the playboy   127

10   High points   139

11   Low points   149

12   Followers   171

13   Money   181

Career records   191

Acknowledgements   199

Chapter 1

Messi and Cristiano, Cristiano and Messi

Team Messi or Team Cristiano? Choosing a side seems more or less obligatory these days. The footballing world is divided – although it's not an easy choice. It's about more than just the stats and the trophies, it's about deep-seated loyalties and the emotions these two players stir up. It's a debate swirling with emotion and passion as much as statistics and reason. Every tiny detail is analysed and compared: gestures, on-the-pitch behaviour, dribbling technique, fouls, assists, goals, matches, championships, prizes, their most recent statements, the latest research.

CR7 versus Messi has earned its place as a classic derby. Sport is fuelled by rivalries between athletes, teams and countries, as well as by comparisons between different periods in each of their histories. Memory is a fundamental element of the game and pitting one person against another is a favourite pastime which has always divided world media opinion. Boxers Ali and Foreman, racing drivers Prost and Senna, tennis stars

Borg and McEnroe, basketball players Magic Johnson and Larry Bird, motorcycle racers Valentino Rossi and Marc Márquez, athletes Carl Lewis and Ben Johnson ... But in football it is rare to find a player considered to be a 'great' who can also be overshadowed by a contemporary. Pelé, Cruyff, Maradona and Di Stéfano never overlapped in terms of their time at the top. But now there is a personal duel between two stars which has become a one-on-one ever since the Portuguese player arrived in La Liga.

Which brings us to the most frequently asked question: who is the best? It's a question asked over and over in the newspapers, on the radio, on TV and on blogs, and everyone from coaches, footballers and pundits to plain old fans have been swept up in the debate. Everyone has their own opinion. During his tenure as England coach, Fabio Capello once said: 'It's difficult to decide which one is better. They are both very good but in different ways. Messi is unpredictable, no one is capable of doing what he does. But Cristiano is very powerful and has incredible speed.' But when asked who he would choose for his squad, Capello joked: 'Cristiano speaks English. But Messi speaks football.'

Former Argentina coach Sergio 'El Checho' Batista agrees with the *Economist*: 'For me, Messi is the best, but both of them are up there on the list of greats. Leo has amazing skills, he's incredibly talented, and he has a left-footed shot that many players envy. Cristiano hits the ball very well, he is strong and he moves very fast.' Pep Guardiola is even more emphatic, insisting that Leo is the best player in history. 'There has never been a player like him, and I don't think there will ever be another like him,' the Manchester City manager has said.

There are some who refuse to be drawn on the matter. 'They are both top players,' says former Portugal manager Paulo Bento. 'If they didn't play in the same country there wouldn't be a debate about who was better.' And then there are others who are die-hard Cristiano fans no matter what. 'He is a more complete player than Messi, in the sense that he plays equally well with both feet, and his head,' points out CD Castellón and former Valencia player Ángel Dealbert. 'He can push forward and he can shoot. Messi loses points when it comes to headers and playing with the right foot.' Carlo Ancelotti also needs no convincing: 'Cristiano is from another world. He scores with incredible ease. It's difficult to find the words to describe him.' As if that's not enough, the Bayern Munich manager adds: 'No disrespect to anyone else, but Cristiano is the best footballer I have ever coached.' Even Usain Bolt is a big fan of the Portuguese. 'Ronaldo is better than Messi, without a doubt. He's a more well-rounded player,' says the champion athlete, adding: 'Plus he's fun and he's a great person.' And of course, we have to hear from Sir Alex Ferguson. 'People say, "Who's the best player in the world?" and plenty of people rightly say Lionel Messi – you can't dispute that opinion. But Ronaldo could play for Millwall, Queens Park Rangers and Doncaster and score a hat-trick. I'm not sure Messi could do it. Ronaldo's got two feet, quick, brave in the air. I think Messi's a Barcelona player.'

Ever since the two stars went head to head they have always been portrayed as opponents, and the press and fans have drawn attention to the rivalry ever since CR7 moved to Real Madrid. They are viewed as great enemies as much as great stars. Each the kryptonite to the other's Superman. Ronaldo's fans and detractors always seem to fixate on Messi – and vice versa. Whenever fans from any team across the world want to attempt to rile one of them, they shout the other's name. And in interviews, each is constantly asked his opinion of the other.

Nevertheless, in public at least, the two have always shown the utmost respect for each other. 'We're colleagues. We're friends professionally, although obviously we don't spend time together outside the realm of football. The same goes for my relationship with other players,' Ronaldo has explained. 'He works hard to play the best that he can for his club and country, just as I do. There's a certain rivalry in that we each want the best for our teams. I hope that in a few years' time we'll look back and laugh about it together. Football is a game, it's entertainment, something that makes us happy. It's a beautiful thing, something everyone in the world enjoys. We have to approach the rivalry with a positive attitude, because it's a good thing.' The presence of someone like Messi has pushed CR7 to ever greater heights. And the Argentine has a similar opinion: 'There is no real rivalry, there never has been. It's something the press like to hype up. We both just want to do the best that we can for our clubs. It's not Messi versus Ronaldo, it never has been.'

In truth, there was a slight tension in the early days whenever they crossed paths during a match or public appearance. But in recent seasons they have been very relaxed about it, even exchanging private remarks or gestures, as they did at the Ballon d'Or ceremony in January 2015. The maturity that has developed on the pitch over the years has been reflected in the real world. But make no mistake, they each want the same thing: to triumph over the other. They are hungry for victory, passionate, indefatigable. They have the drive to constantly improve and the will to succeed.

They are always convinced that victory is just within their reach and they just need the confidence and determination to make it happen. Neither one ever gives up, they know that success requires discipline and sacrifice. What they have in common is their ability to put their feelings aside and give 200 per cent to the task in hand. They have the talent and the skills, they are natural goal-scorers, the real deal. But they are also two professionals obsessed with their profession, seeking perfection.

Who is the best? This book doesn't try to answer that. But it will tell you everything you need to know about these two footballing superstars to make up your own mind.

Chapter 2

The Rosarino versus the Madeiran

Cristiano and Leo are two of the highest-paid sportsmen in the world, but they were not always accustomed to such a life of luxury. They are both from modest, working-class families, for whom making ends meet was often a challenge.

The Real Madrid star is born on 5 February 1985 at 10.20am at the Cruz de Carvalho Hospital in Funchal, the capital of Madeira, an island in the Atlantic Ocean, some 860 kilometres from Lisbon. He weighs 4 kilos. He is the fourth child of María Dolores dos Santos and José Dinis Aveiro, joining Hugo, Elma and Katia. The family's three-bedroom concrete council house in Quinta do Falcão would later be demolished in 2007 to avoid problems with squatters.

They had not planned to have another child. Katia is already nine years old, and this latest pregnancy took them by surprise. Nonetheless CR7 quickly becomes the spoiled baby of the family. The first thing they need to do is come up with a name. 'My sister, who was working in an orphanage at the time, said that if it was a boy we could name him Cristiano,' recalls Dolores. 'I thought it was a good choice. And my husband and I both liked the name Ronaldo, after Ronald Reagan. My sister chose Cristiano and we chose Ronaldo.'

Just over two years later, thousands of miles away, Celia Cuccittini is admitted to the maternity ward of the Garibaldi Hospital in the Argentine town of Rosario, the largest town in Santa Fe province. Seven-year-old Rodrigo and five-year-old Matías are waiting at home with their grandmother, while their father Jorge Messi accompanies their mother to the hospital. The pregnancy has been uneventful, but during the final few hours complications arise. Gynaecologist Norberto Odetto diagnoses severe foetal distress and decides to induce labour in order to avoid any lasting effects on the baby. To this day, Jorge can recall the fear of those moments, the panic he felt when the doctor told him that he was going to use forceps, his plea that he do everything possible to avoid using those pincers, which, as is the case with many parents, concerned him greatly due to the horror stories he had heard regarding deformity and damage to one's baby. In the end the forceps are not needed, and Lionel Andrés Messi is born a few minutes after 6.00am on 24 June 1987. Now that the initial fears have passed, they can celebrate. The new arrival is a healthy 3 kilos.

Leo grows up in the home that Jorge has built at

weekends with the help of his father Eusebio. It's a brick house on a 300 square-metre plot, with a backyard where the children can play, and it's in the Las Heras neighbourhood in southern Rosario, home to humble, hardworking people. Jorge is the head of department at a steelmaking company, while Celia works at a magnet manufacturing workshop.

Over in Madeira, Cristiano's father Dinis is the town hall gardener, while Dolores works hard as a cook so that she can put food on the table for her own children as well. Like thousands of Portuguese citizens, Dolores had emigrated to France at the age of twenty, where she spent three months cleaning houses. Her husband was going to join her, but when he wasn't able to she returned to Madeira. They already had two children. Life isn't easy for the Aveiro family. It's tough for anyone who lives far away from the luxury hotel industry which has colonised the coast. It's a small home for a family of six – and whenever there's a storm the house leaks in dozens of places. Dolores fetches bricks and mortar from the town hall to try to keep the problem under control. But today, Cristiano remembers that time as a happy childhood. At two or three years old, playing in the yard or on Lombinho Street, he began to discover his best friend – the football.

'One Christmas I gave him a remote-control car, thinking that would keep him busy,' recalls his godfather Fernão Sousa, 'but he preferred to play with a football. He slept with his ball, it never left his side. It was always under his arm – wherever he went, it went with him.'

Ronaldo's love of football has been handed down through the family. In his spare time, Dinis was a kit man for local team Andorinha. And it's no surprise when he chooses the team's captain to be little Cristiano's godfather. In fact, Dinis and Fernão Sousa are more than half an hour late to the baptism because they don't want to miss Andorinha's match against Ribeira Brava.

'From the day he walked through the door, football was Cristiano's favourite sport,' recalls María dos Santos, one of his former teachers. 'He took part in other activities, learnt songs and did his work, but he liked to have time for himself, time for football. If there wasn't a real ball around – and often there wasn't – he would make one out of socks. He would always find a way of playing football in the playground. I don't know how he managed it.'

Cristiano has to play in the street because there is no pitch near his house. One particular street, Quinta do Falcão, proves to be a challenge when buses, cars and motorbikes want to get through. He and his friends have to remove the stones marking out the goalposts each time and wait for the traffic to pass before resuming the game. Their games are intense battles between households, between gangs of friends. They are games that never end. There's a well where Cristiano spends hours on end kicking the ball against the wall alone. The well and the street are his first training grounds. It's here, between the pavement, the asphalt and the cars, playing against kids young and old, that Ronaldo learns the tricks and techniques which will make him great and become the hallmarks of his signature style. 'He used to spend all day in the street, doing authentic tricks with the ball. It was as if it was attached to his foot,' recalls Adelino Andrade, who lived near the Aveiro family. 'When it came to football he was truly gifted,' maintains Cristiano's sister, Elma. 'But we never dreamed he would be where he is today.'

It takes Leo a bit longer to discover his love of football. At three years old, the Flea, as he is known, prefers picture cards and much smaller balls – marbles. He wins multitudes of them from his playmates and his bag is always full. At nursery or at school there is always time to play with round objects. For his fourth birthday, his parents give him a white ball with red diamonds. It is then, perhaps, that the fatal attraction begins. Until one day he surprises everyone. His father and brothers are playing in the street and Leo decides to join the game for the first time. On many other occasions he had preferred to keep winning marbles – but not this time. 'We were stunned when we saw what he could do,' says Jorge. 'He had never played before.'

From that moment on there is no turning back. Football is to become his whole life, just as it has become

Cristiano's, although both players stumble into their first 'official' match purely by chance. In fact, there are a lot of similarities in the circumstances. They both go along as spectators, and end up on the pitch. Cristiano's cousin and best mate Nuno plays for Andorinha. One day he invites him to come and watch a match, and asks if he wants to put on the sky-blue shirt. Cristiano joins the practice and decides to stick around. He is just six years old, and three years later he will be awarded his first sporting licence, number 17,182 in the Funchal football association. Meanwhile he earns the nickname *Abelhinha*, 'Little Bee', as he buzzes non-stop around the pitch. 'He was fast, he was technically brilliant and he played equally well with his left and right foot,' says Francisco Afonso, Ronaldo's former primary school teacher and first coach. 'He was skinny but he was a head taller than other kids his age. He was undoubtedly extremely gifted – he had a natural talent that was in the genes. He was always chasing the ball, he wanted to be the one to finish the game. He was very focused, he worked equally hard regardless of where he was on the pitch. And whenever he couldn't play or he missed a game he was devastated.'

That same year, over in Rosario, Leo's grandmother has been going every Tuesday and Thursday to watch grandsons Rodrigo and Matías train at the Grandoli ground. One summer afternoon, Leo decides to go with them. The coach at that time was Salvador Ricardo Aparicio, aka Don Apa, who passed away at the age of 80. He never forgot the first time he saw the Flea. 'I needed one more to complete the '86 team,' he recalled whenever anyone asked him how he discovered the Barça star. 'I was waiting for the final player with the shirt in my hands while the others were warming up. But he didn't show up and there was this little kid kicking the ball against the stands. The cogs were turning and I said to myself, damn ... I don't know if he knows how to play but ... So I went to speak to the grandmother, who was really into football, and I said to her: "Lend him to me." She wanted to see him on the pitch. She had asked me many times to let him try out. On many occasions she would tell me about all the little guy's talents. The mother, or the aunt, I can't remember which, didn't want him to play: "He's so small, the others are all huge." To reassure her I told her: "I'll stand him over here, and if they attack him I'll stop the game and take him off."

'Well, I gave him the shirt and he put it on. The first ball came his way, he looked at it and ... nothing. He's left-footed, that's why he didn't get to the ball. The second it came to his left foot, he latched on to it, and went past one guy, then another and another. I was yelling at him: "Kick it, kick it." He was terrified someone would hurt him but he kept going and going. I don't remember if he scored the goal – I had never seen anything like it. I said to myself: "That one's never coming off." And I never took him off.'

And so begin Cristiano and Leo's sporting careers. Long before their teens, they are both firmly established in the youth leagues, Messi at Newell's Old Boys, and Ronaldo at Nacional da Madeira. They are light years ahead of the rest and are soon catching the scouts' attention. 'Cristiano's skills were already highly developed: speed, dribbling, shooting, lightning execution. Street football had taught him how to avoid getting hit, sidestep the opponent and face up to kids much bigger than he was. It had also strengthened his character – he was extremely courageous,' says António Mendoça, Cristiano's coach during his two seasons playing in black and white. 'Leo was something special,' recalls Ernesto Vecchio, Messi's second coach at Newell's. 'He had wisdom, he could sprint, his passes were spot on; he played for his teammates, but he was capable of going past half the opposing team. Once on the Malvinas School of Football first pitch, the goalie passed him the ball in defence and he ran the length of the pitch and went on to score an incredible goal. He didn't need to be taught a thing. What can you teach to a Maradona or a Pelé? There are only very tiny things for a coach to correct.'

Now all that remains is to make the crucial journey across the pond to mainland Europe, where CR7 will join Sporting Lisbon, and the Flea will head for FC Barcelona.

Chapter 3

30–22

When it comes to clubs their CVs are rather different – Ronaldo has played for three teams while Messi has stuck with one. It seems like a minor detail, but it is actually quite significant. Would Leo have found it easier to integrate if he had had the chance to experience various different dressing rooms? Can CR7's alleged arrogance be attributed to having played in three different national championships? Each player's journey has undoubtedly had an impact on who they are and their achievements to date. Let's retrace their steps …

2002–03 Season

Sporting is Cristiano's home, it has shaped who he is today. The Lisbon club gave him his first real chance to shine, and was prepared to let him go when he was ready to become a star.

On 1 July 2002, the moment Cristiano has been waiting for finally arrives when he becomes a first team player. He has the backing of Romanian coach László Bölöni, former star midfielder for Steaua Bucharest, who beat Barcelona to the European Cup in 1986. Ronaldo shines in the first few pre-season matches, and the coach makes a few adjustments. The kid is used to playing up front, but the manager puts him on the left wing – he can make good use of his speed there, but it's also better because he's not physically up to taking on the opposition defenders yet.

He doesn't disappoint. He is fast, he has good ball control and he creates trouble for his markers. 'This boy is one to watch,' writes Portuguese sports paper *Record*. 'He knows how to lose his opponent, he can dribble, and he has a nose for goals.' And the boy in question has plenty to say after a pre-season match against Paris Saint-Germain: 'The shareholders have yet to see the real Ronaldo. This is just the beginning.' He is cheeky, irreverent and very sure of himself. And he is only seventeen years old.

On 14 August 2002 he plays his first competitive match for the Lions against Inter Milan in a Champions League qualifier. Nothing spectacular, but he puts in a good all-round performance. Just one criticism – he makes a bit too much of his solo runs and one-on-one duels. It's a youthful affectation that will take a few years to correct.

He is certainly capable of entertaining the crowds, and he proves it in his second outing, on 7 October in the Portuguese SuperLiga. The current title holders are at home to Moreirense FC, who have been promoted from the second division. Cristiano is in the starting line-up for the first time, and at seventeen years, eight months and two days old he makes history as Sporting's youngest ever goal-scorer. He scores 'a monumental, majestic, unbelievable goal ... there are not sufficient adjectives to describe this young Sporting prodigy's achievement', scream the SportTV commentators.

It's the 34th minute: Ronaldo gets a backheel from Toñito just over the halfway line, he dodges past two defenders, slaloming back and forth for some 60 metres; he follows it up with a stepover on the edge of the area to wrong-foot another opponent and slides it smoothly past Moreirense goalkeeper João Ricardo, who makes a desperate dash out into the box. But he's not done yet. He also goes on to make it a comprehensive 3–0 with a spectacular header. The following day the press are raving about him – and not just in Portugal. Italy's *La Gazzetta dello Sport* dedicates its front page to the 'new Ronaldo', comparing him with Brazil's Ronaldo Nazario da Lima, the Portuguese's favourite player, who at the time is at Real Madrid.

Cristiano's performances in the Lions' first team have been outstanding. He has become the fans' golden boy. But there is a lot of competition up front at Sporting, and by the end of the season he has only started in eleven matches. It hasn't been a great run for the team. They have failed to qualify for the Champions League group stages, having been beaten 2–0 by Inter in the return leg at the San Siro. They are also out of the UEFA Cup, after losing 1–3 to Serbia's FK Partizan in Portugal and drawing 3–3 in the second leg. On 1 May 2003 they are knocked out of the Portugal Cup by Naval in the quarter-finals. And they fail to hold on to their league title.

They finish third, 27 points behind José Mourinho's Porto and sixteen behind Benfica. The season has been something of a washout for the club, but it has been nothing short of life-changing for the young Portuguese player.

2003–04 Season

His move to Manchester United was almost inevitable. The Red Devils have had an ongoing agreement with Sporting for quite a while now. The youth academy at Alcochete has become like a surrogate academy for United – they have first option on any promising Sporting youngsters, and the Lisbon club must inform them of any outside interest. Nonetheless, the negotiations have been top secret. No one wants the news to get out until after the friendly between the two clubs to inaugurate the Lions' new stadium. On 6 August 2003, Cristiano goes out on to the pitch to show the Man United fans just what he can do. He is wearing number 28, and it will be his best match at Sporting. He is off to a flying start and makes the United defenders suffer on the wing. He tests United goalkeeper Fabien

Barthez's limits, with shots from afar and a one-on-one which the French goalie wins. In the 25th minute he serves up the ball for Luís Filipe to score the first goal. But above all, he amazes everyone with his dribbling, speed, stepovers, changes of pace and ability to evade his opponents.

Back in the United dressing room, everyone is telling Sir Alex Ferguson that they have to sign the Portuguese. The coach stays quiet. He has no intention of announcing to his players that the deal is all but done. He's a sly fox. He wants the kid to be accepted in the dressing room from day one, and what better way to do that than to allow them to think that they had something to do with bringing him over from Sporting.

A week after the friendly (which ends 3–1 to Sporting), Cristiano arrives in Manchester to meet Ferguson. He is convinced he will sign the contract, have a medical, visit Old Trafford and take a look around the facilities and then return to Lisbon for a year on loan to Sporting. But Ferguson has other plans. Once he has arrived and has signed the contract (€2 million a year – more than €150,000 a month compared to the €2,000 he was making at Sporting), Ferguson sits down with Cristiano's agent Jorge Mendes. 'I didn't understand any of the English,' Cristiano tells Portuguese newspaper *Público* years later. 'Mendes explained to me that Ferguson wanted me to stay in Manchester. I was shocked and nervous.' He doesn't know what to do – he hasn't even brought his belongings. He is due to start his training out in Carrington, and go back later and get his things.

On 13 August, the day of his presentation, not everyone has positive things to say about the newcomer. Ronaldo is the most expensive teenager in the history of British football. Fifteen million Euros seems like a lot for an eighteen-year-old with only 25 top division matches and three goals under his belt. But Ferguson has taken a risk and time will show he is right. The kid will wear number 7, worn by all the United greats before him: George Best, Steve Coppell, Bryan Robson, Eric Cantona and David Beckham. How is it possible that a new signing who is so young gets to wear a shirt that carries the weight of the club's history? Ronaldo will later recount to the *Sun* what happened. 'I asked whether the number 28 shirt, which I had at Sporting Lisbon, was available. Alex Ferguson said to me, "No no, yours is the number 7." "OK boss!" I said. I wasn't going to say to him, "No no, mine is the number 28."' Incidentally, 7 is also a special number for Cristiano, as it was the number worn by his great Sporting predecessor Luís Figo.

Ronaldo debuts at Old Trafford three days after his official presentation. It is the first game of the season and Man United are at home to Bolton. Cristiano is on the bench, but in the 60th minute Ferguson needs to shake up a game that is stuck at 1–0 and he sends him on as a substitute for Nicky Butt. The spectators stand to applaud the new signing, while the commentators remind viewers that he is 'one of the most expensive teenagers in the game'. The 67,647 fans certainly aren't disappointed by his running and dribbling, and during the remaining 30 minutes the new number 7 demonstrates his potential on the wing. He creates two chances and wins a penalty, which van Nistelrooy fails to convert. He is crowned man of the match and gets to pop his first bottle of champagne. Roy Keane is the first to congratulate him, followed by his other teammates, and he receives a standing ovation from the crowd.

But it is just the beginning of a long season, one in which he has to adapt to a much more physical style of play, and in which Man United will disappoint, finishing third in the Premier League behind Arsenal and Chelsea, and with only the FA Cup to their name. In the final against Millwall, Ronaldo scores one of their three goals, and he is instrumental in the attack. He isn't the man of the match, but everyone is talking about him. He finishes his first season on a high. He has scored eight goals in 39 appearances across all the various tournaments. And with more than 10,000 votes from the Man United fans, he is named the Sir Matt Busby Player of the Year.

That same season, another young player is starting out on his journey to the top. The date 16 November 2003 will forever be etched in Lionel Messi's memory.

He is just sixteen years, four months and 23 days old when he steps out on to the pitch with Barcelona's first team for the first time. They are playing Porto in a friendly to mark the inauguration of the new Dragão Stadium. He comes on in the 74th minute and plays for fifteen minutes, creating two chances at goal.

2004–05 Season

Less than a year later, on 26 October 2004, Leo plays in his first competitive match, becoming the youngest in Barça history to play in La Liga (a record that will later be broken by Bojan Krkić). But he will have to wait until 1 May 2005 to score his first goal. It happens in the 34th round of Liga matches. The Nou Camp scoreboard shows three minutes remaining, and the *Blaugrana* are 1–0 up over Albacete. Coach Frank Rijkaard brings off Samuel Eto'o, sending Messi on in the unusual position of centre forward. The little guy takes advantage of an assist from Ronaldinho and chips the ball over goalie Valbuena's head to score. He is just two months shy of his eighteenth birthday, and he has just become the youngest ever goal-scorer in La Liga history (another record that will be toppled by Krkić, on 20 October 2007 with a strike against Villareal).

Across the Channel it has been a slow season for Cristiano. It takes him until 5 December 2004 to score his first Premier League goal, at home to Southampton. 'He has promised us twelve goals, and hopefully that's the start of them,' says Ferguson. But Cristiano can only manage nine goals in 50 matches. It's an equally disappointing season for United, who finish trophyless as Chelsea claim the league title.

2005–06 Season

Cristiano's third season in England is a tough one, both on and off the pitch. He loses his goal-scoring bet with Ferguson once again, having said he would net fifteen goals and finishing with twelve. At least it's close. He's clearly making progress, but United finish behind José Mourinho's Chelsea for the second season running, and they are knocked out of the Champions League in the group stages. The only trophy to their name is the Carling Cup. They beat Wigan 4–0 in the final, with the third from Ronaldo.

On 29 October 2005 Cristiano scores a header against Middlesbrough in extra time – Man United's thousandth Premier League goal. Unfortunately they go on to lose 4–1. But despite his team's run of bad luck, the fans name Ronaldo their young player of the year.

This is the year Leo will play his first *Clásico* against Real Madrid. And 19 November will go down in history for the fans' incredible ovation to Ronaldinho for his two goals, and for a spectacular match in general. On top of that Messi makes his mark by serving up the first goal for Eto'o and initiating some outstanding moves.

But his truly standout match is to come on 22 February 2006, in the first leg of the Champions League last-sixteen tie against Chelsea. He looks like a little boy as he heads out on to the pitch, but he's about to be the man of the match. He runs up and down, stealing balls, passing accurately, working well with his teammates, creating the first real chance and sowing the seeds of panic among the Chelsea defence. The *Blaugrana* win thanks to a single Eto'o goal, but their opponents' rage is all directed towards Leo: Mourinho blames him for Asier Del Horno's sending off, which has left his team a man down. 'What can we do? Ask for them to retract Del Horno's red card? Suspend Messi for his theatrics? Nothing will change the result ... Because let's be serious, Messi put on an act. Catalonia is a country of culture, you know it is. And I've been to the theatre many times and it's very high quality over there. And Messi has learnt from the best ...'

Luck is not on Lionel's side in the return leg on 7 March. In the 23rd minute he steals the ball from Robben – but suddenly he puts his hand to his left knee and falls to the ground. He'll be out for 79 days, watching the Champions League final from the stands at the Stade de France in Paris. His teammates beat Arsenal to clinch the trophy, and go up to lift the cup for the second time in Barça's history. Sad and alone, Leo does not go down to the pitch to collect his medal.

2006–07 Season

Nearly a year on, Messi is not only fully recovered, he has transformed into Fabio Capello's worst nightmare. The Real Madrid coach has never won at the Nou Camp, not with Juventus, Roma or Real. It looks like he might be about to break that drought on 10 March 2007 ... but he has reckoned without the Flea, who bursts on to the scene once, twice, persistently bringing the scores level. And then, in the 90th minute, just when it looks like the Whites have it in the bag, he pulls the most beautiful move out of his hat, the speediest run and a low shot into the corner to make it 3–3. Capello and his men are like children who have had their lollipop snatched from their mouths. A month later he astounds everyone with a fabulous goal against Getafe in the Copa del Rey.

While Leo is lighting up La Liga, Cristiano is having his best season so far at United. It's a year of self-improvement, in which he has managed to detach himself from previous tabloid harassment and focus on giving the best possible performances. First there had been accusations of rape but he was cleared of all charges. Then there was controversy surrounding a Portugal–England match in the 2006 FIFA World Cup in Germany, which ended with Rooney's expulsion and England's exit. 'I managed to show that the pressure only makes me stronger,' he says later. On 22 April 2007 he is named the Professional Footballers' Association

Player of the Year and Young Player of the Year. And he finally gets his hands on the Premier League trophy. The Red Devils' number 7 has played his part as the third-highest scorer in the league with sixteen goals.

2007–08 Season

And his hunger for goals only increases. The following year he is the top scorer with 31. One particular stand-out match is on 12 January 2008 against Newcastle, where he scores his first hat-trick for United. And two months later Ferguson gives him the captain's armband. He finishes the season as the PFA Player of the Year and a Premier League champion with United once again. But this time there are two more trophies for the cabinet: the Charity Shield, and United's third European Cup. As Cristiano lifts the cup, he can also celebrate his personal achievements as the best player and top goal-scorer of the competition with eight to his name.

He has had his disappointments as well. In the Champions League final against Chelsea in Moscow on 21 May 2008, he puts United ahead with a majestic header in the 26th minute. But the Blues pull it back a few seconds before the break, and the match ends up going to extra time, followed by penalties. Carlos Tévez is first up and he makes it 1–0 to United. Next it's Michael Ballack: 1–1. Both Michael Carrick and Juliano Belletti convert theirs to take it to 2–2. The third penalty falls to the number 7. Ronaldo kisses the ball and places it carefully on the penalty spot. He puts his hands on his hips as always, lowers his head, takes a deep breath and waits for the referee's whistle. He takes his run-up, opting for the Brazilian-style 'paradinha', the little stop intended to confuse the goalie. Petr Čech anticipates the move and still manages to block the shot. Cristiano buries his face in his hands and slowly walks away, devastated. He is not the first great player in history to falter at the moment of truth, but at the moment it seems like the darkest day of his life. But luck is still on his side as Chelsea's Terry and Anelka miss, sealing the victory for United. 'In the end it was the happiest day of my life,' he says later.

Meanwhile it's a sad end to the season for Leo, as Barcelona finish without a single title. He has made a good impression on the pitch for the majority of the year, and the murmurs have begun about him being the best in the world and a potential Ballon d'Or candidate. But on 4 March 2008 he sustains a thigh injury in the second leg of the Champions League last-sixteen tie against Celtic, putting him out for a month and a half. He finishes with ten goals in La Liga and six in the Champions League.

2008–09 Season
The following year the luck begins to swing in his favour. Cristiano and the Flea come face to face in

the Champions League final at the Olympic Stadium in Rome on 27 May 2009. Barça dominate, beating United 2–0. Despite retaining the Premier League title and beating Tottenham in the final of the Carling Cup, Ronaldo has lost his final match in a Man United shirt. On 6 July 2009 he is presented as Real Madrid's new star signing in front of 80,000 fans at the Santiago Bernabéu. He has cost the Whites £80 million, a new world record.

It's a happier year for Messi, as Barça become the first Spanish team to win the treble: La Liga, the Champions League and the Copa del Rey. Only five European clubs have won all of the top three titles available to them in the same season – the most recent being Man United. Leo has scored more goals than ever before in his professional career. Twenty-three in La Liga, making him the fourth-highest scorer after Diego Forlán, Samuel Eto'o and David Villa. And let's not forget the 5,000th goal in the Catalan club's Liga history, which Leo scores on 1 February 2009 in Santander against Racing. It is his second of the match, and secures a victory for Barça. There are six more in the Copa del Rey, in which he is the tournament's top goal-scorer, despite only playing 452 minutes (an average of a goal every 75 minutes), as well as two in the Spanish Super Cup. And nine goals in the Champions League make him the highest goal-scorer in the European tournament. In contrast to the previous two years, he does not sustain even a minor injury in all his 51 matches. 'It has been an incredible year. I have thoroughly enjoyed it,' enthuses the star, who, to top it all off, comes second in the race for FIFA World Player of the Year ... behind Cristiano Ronaldo. Twelve months later, he will knock him off the top spot.

2009–10 Season
The Flea is unstoppable. On 19 December 2009 Barcelona finally win their first Club World Cup, after coming close in 1992 (when it was the Intercontinental Cup) and 2006. They beat Estudiantes de La Plata, and Messi scores with his chest – his heart, the emblem on his shirt. He gets away from his Argentine friend Juan Sebastián Verón and converts Dani Alves' cross in the 110th minute with an effort off the chest that no one is expecting. It's 2–1 at the final whistle, and the *Blaugrana* are crowned kings of the world. No team has ever won six titles in one calendar year before, but now Barça have won the Club World Cup, Champions League, European Super Cup, Spanish Super Cup, Copa del Rey and La Liga.

And as if that's not enough, Leo breaks another record on 16 January 2010, against Sevilla in La Liga, becoming the youngest Barça player to score 100 goals. He is just 22½. Three months later he becomes the first *Blaugrana* player to score four goals in a Champions

League match as they beat Arsenal 4–1 in the second leg of the quarter-finals. By the end of the season he has racked up 46 goals across all competitions, including nine doubles and four hat-tricks. And with 34 La Liga goals he has equalled the tally of the Brazilian Ronaldo in 1996–97 when he played at Barcelona. The Flea has beaten all his previous tallies since he joined the first team six seasons ago. The only low point is that they are knocked out of the Champions League in the semi-finals by José Mourinho's Inter Milan.

For CR7, the season leaves much to be desired, but not because of the level of his performance. In fact, he gets off to a flying start, the best of his whole career, scoring seven goals in his first five matches. By the end he has scored 33 in total, despite being out injured for two months. He has netted 26 in La Liga (including his first hat-trick for Real against Mallorca on 5 May 2010) and seven in the Champions League. He has entertained the Bernabéu crowds and won the hearts of the fans. But he has a right to be frustrated: Real have had a dud season. They have not made it further than the last sixteen in the Champions League or the Copa del Rey, and La Liga has been all about Barcelona.

2010–11 Season

It's much the same for the Portuguese the following season. Cristiano is becoming an unstoppable goal-scoring machine, netting a total of 53 goals and winning the award for top goal-scorer in Europe. And with his 40 La Liga goals in 34 matches he smashes the records set by Athletic Bilbao's Telmo Zarra, who scored 38 goals in 30 matches in the 1950–51 season, and Real's own Hugo Sánchez, who scored 38 in 35 matches in the 1989–90 season.

But once again the Whites only manage one title, beating Barcelona to the Copa del Rey. It's clearly not enough for someone with the Portuguese's sense of ambition. 'Real aspires to win all the titles and I would have preferred to score half the number of goals but win La Liga or the Champions League,' he explains in an interview with the Cadena COPE radio station. On balance, his personal star is on the rise. 'I have felt a lot more comfortable and you could even say this has been my best season.' He gives his performance and that of the team an eight or nine out of ten. But there's no denying that Real and Cristiano have had a diffi- cult year thanks to their eternal rivals: Pep Guardiola's Barcelona and, above all, Leo Messi.

Leo has pushed himself to even greater heights, equalling Cristiano's total goal tally of 53. In the Champions League, he is in the lead: twelve goals, equalling Ruud van Nistelrooy's record – the Dutchman scored the same number with Man United in 2002–03. Twenty-three years of age, top Champions League scorer for the third time, not to mention winner of fourteen trophies with Barcelona. But statistics and silverware aside, it is worth noting that when it matters most, Messi is there; he is always a game-changer and he always plays to the best of his abilities. He is a crucial factor in his team's third consecutive Liga victory.

And perhaps more importantly, he gets to lift his third Champions League trophy on 29 May 2011 at Wembley, after beating Man United yet again. At the home of English football, the Flea leads a wonderfully lively performance, exquisite and lyrical, and the Brits leave the ground knowing that they have just witnessed a supreme exhibition of the 'beautiful game'. A match to tell their grandchildren about and a man-of-the-match performance which exhausts all the media's best adjectives. *The Times* proclaims: 'King Messi reigns'. The *Guardian* compares it to Nándor Hidegkuti's performance at the same stadium, when he scored a hat-trick in Hungary's 6–3 victory over England in the autumn of 1953. On this occasion, the final score is a convincing 3–1. 'He is the best player I have ever seen, and will ever see,' says Pep Guardiola after the final. 'We could compete at a very high level, but without him we wouldn't be able to play such a high-quality game. We have demonstrated that we are capable of working very hard, we have talent, and we have Messi. He is a unique and irreplaceable footballer.'

2011–12 Season

Leo really is an extraordinary player, and he is deci-sive once again in Barça's win over Real Madrid in the Spanish Super Cup in August 2011. He scores in both the home and away legs, sealing the club's tenth win in the competition (3–1 on aggregate). And he overtakes Raúl González as top scorer in the tournament, with eight. Real coach Mourinho reacts to his team's loss by poking Guardiola's right-hand man Tito Vilanova in the eye. In the same month, the Flea is the first to score against Porto in the European Super Cup, and Cesc Fàbregas gets in on the act to make it one more for the trophy cabinet. In Japan in December, they retain the Club World Cup, beating Neymar's Santos from Brazil. Messi scores two and is named player of the tournament.

And Lionel is on a roll, breaking record after record. On 18 January 2012 he makes his 300th appearance for the *Blaugrana*. Coincidentally it is against his eternal rivals, Real Madrid, in the first leg of the Copa del Rey. On 7 March he obliterates Bayer Leverkusen with five goals in the second leg of the Champions League last sixteen, in what will go on to be a 7–1 humiliation. The last person to score five in a European Cup match was Danish footballer Søren Lerby in the 1979–80 season for Ajax against Greek club AC Omonia – and no one has done it since it became the UEFA Champions League. And on 20 March he becomes the highest goal-scorer in Barcelona history, with 234 goals in 315 matches. He seals it with a hat-trick against Granada in the 29th league match of the season.

But despite these incredible stats, his happiness is incomplete. On 24 April he stumbles when least expected, missing a crucial penalty that could have put Barça through to the final of the Champions League. They are playing Chelsea at the Nou Camp. In the first leg at Stamford Bridge, a goal from Drogba broke their concentration and they lost 1–0. Now, in the rematch, everyone is looking to Messi, who has never scored against the Blues in all his seven encounters against them. It's 1–1 at half-time. When the game resumes, Drogba fouls Fàbregas in the box and the referee gives the penalty. Petr Čech spreads his long arms to defend his goal, as Messi steps up to the penalty spot looking serious. He shoots. Čech throws himself to his left. But the Flea has aimed too high and the ball rebounds off the crossbar. It's a major blow for both Messi and Barça. At the final whistle, he buries his face in his shirt. It has been his worst night for some time. It doesn't matter that he is the Champions League top goal-scorer for the fourth year running, equalling Gerd Müller's 1970s record.

The Champions League has slipped from his grasp, and so does La Liga. It's Cristiano's turn to win their duel at the Nou Camp, sealing the championship for Real. It is one of the Portuguese's best performances at his rivals' home ground. He scores Real's second to make it 1–2, and can finally enjoy his first Liga trophy. 'It's a feeling of great joy – I'm so happy. The fans deserve it,' he says later, during the celebrations with the Real fans at the Plaza de Cibeles in Madrid.

But barely four days after the Liga win against Barcelona, the magic has already evaporated. Despite the Portuguese's two goals in the second leg of the Champions League semi-final against Bayern Munich, the match goes to penalties ... and Cristiano misses. Just like Messi did. At the crucial moment, Cristiano has missed the penalty that could have put Real on an entirely different path. But unlike Messi, he has made his mark during the previous 120 minutes. He scored a penalty in the sixth minute and another in the fourteenth. Then, with Real 2–0 up, he moved ten paces back, waiting for the Germans to falter in order to then go on the counterattack. It's a conservative strategy from Mourinho, which fails them in the end, despite goalie Íker Casillas's best efforts. Robben scores a penalty, which takes them on to the shootout. Goodbye Champions League.

2012–13 Season

Ronaldo starts the new season downcast. Despite beating Barça to the Spanish Super Cup in August, and becoming the only player to score in six consecutive *Clásicos*, he isn't celebrating his goals. When the press ask why, he responds mysteriously: 'It could be that I'm a little bit sad. I don't celebrate goals because I'm unhappy.' He refuses to comment further on the matter, and the rumour mill is in overdrive. Is it his strategy to secure a pay rise? Does he want a transfer? Or is he just looking for a little more love from the club? Only at the end of the season does Florentino Pérez offer his version of events. In an interview with Cadena Ser radio station, the Real Madrid president explains: 'Cristiano told me he was unhappy and I told him that we were going to do everything possible to make him happy because he is the best player in the world. I don't know if he had an offer from Paris Saint-Germain. He hit a rough patch, that's it, nothing happened. Lately his performance has been spectacular.'

No one can argue with that, because Cristiano has had a fantastic season. He has scored no fewer than 55 goals in 55 matches, making him the sixth-highest goal-scorer in the club's history. In just four seasons he has overtaken great players such as Amancio Amaro, Emilio Butragueño, Pirri and Paco Gento. And he has been the driving force behind Real Madrid, the hero of many matches, the player with the most guts and enthusiasm, who has pulled the results out of the bag. He has become an authoritative leader on the pitch and in the dressing room and has been ready and willing to take on whatever challenge is thrown his way. Like on 13 February 2013 against Man United in the

Champions League last sixteen. He scores in both the home and away legs to knock out Sir Alex Ferguson's men. It's certainly a satisfying moment, but the 2012–13 season remains trophyless for Real.

Because, once again, La Liga belongs to Messi. The *Blaugrana*'s 22nd Liga title has particular sporting significance. They have dominated the championship from beginning to end. And once again, Leo has exceeded all expectations, despite missing three matches due to injury. On 9 December he scores two against Real Betis in Seville, taking him to a total of 86 goals in 2012 (for club and country), breaking Gerd Müller's 1972 record of 85. The following month, on 27 January 2013, he scores four against Osasuna to reach 200 Liga goals, becoming the youngest player to reach that mark. When Telmo Zarra scored his 200th goal while at Athletic Bilbao back in 1951, he was 29 years and 352 days old. The Flea is four years younger. On 30 March, he scores against Celta Vigo, completing a full cycle of scoring consecutively against every other team in the championship. And on 1 April he equals Alfredo Di Stéfano's record as top goal-scorer in the *Clásicos* between Real Madrid and Barcelona, with eighteen. The *Blaugrana* are knocked out of the Champions League in the semi-finals, but Leo gets to take home his sixth Liga medal. Dummy in the mouth, his son Thiago in his arms: that's the abiding image of Messi during the festivities as Barça celebrate their championship victory. No one could have imagined what was just around the corner ...

2013–14 Season

On 28 September 2013 the Barça number 10 is injured in a match at the Almería ground ... It's the third time he has sustained an injury in less than five months, and it won't be the last. In November he is injured again in a match against Real Betis, after only twenty minutes on the pitch. Speculation is rife about what's going on with the Flea. Some recall that several years back he suffered a catalogue of injuries due to his diet – reportedly fizzy drinks, chocolate and too many Argentine barbecues. Others are fishing for a psychological reason, and some claim that it's all down to a supposed rift in his relationship with Juanjo Brau, who up until now has been his main physiotherapist.

Eight weeks later he is back in the matchday squad for the first leg of a Copa del Rey match against Getafe. He starts on the bench, but comes on in the 61st minute when Barça are already winning 2–0. In 30 minutes he has 36 touches and makes nineteen good passes, has four shots on target and scores two goals. 'He's back with a vengeance,' insists Tata Martino, the club's new Argentine coach. But by the middle of February there are worrying signs once again when he vomits during a match against Real Sociedad in the Copa del Rey. It has happened a few times before: he just doubles over, throws up and continues playing as though nothing has happened. Nonetheless, it's clearly not healthy, and the media and fans are keen to know what's going on. 'I don't know what it is. I have had thousands of tests,' he insists. 'Sometimes it happens before a match. I retch, I end up almost being sick, and then I feel better.' Lacking any official explanation, fans and pundits air their own theories. Some suggest the vomiting could be due to the growth hormones that Leo took until his teens, although the endocrinologist who administered the treatment rejects the possibility of residual effects. Some say it is due to stress caused by nerves during a match, while others think Leo is overexerting himself. The mystery remains unresolved, although that certainly won't stop the conspiracy theories.

On the sporting front, in the same month, Barça lose their hold on La Liga. It's going to be their worst season in quite some time, finishing with only the Spanish Super Cup to their name. The Flea might be the club's top-scoring player of all time, but that's nothing for a footballing genius who is used to winning everything.

And like the theory of yin and yang, just as Leo is taking a bit of a hit, Cristiano Ronaldo is enjoying his time in the spotlight. He is on fire this season. Between 1 September and 19 November he scores no fewer than 34 goals across all competitions, including five hat-tricks. But CR7 demonstrates that he is more than just a prolific goal-scorer. He is a mature and versatile player and a shrewd interpreter of the game. On 10 December at the Parken Stadium, in the final Group B Champions League match against Copenhagen, he sets a new record by being the first player to score nine goals in the group stages. By the end of the year Ronaldo has racked up 69 goals in 59 matches, an average of 1.16 per game and a new personal best.

But despite impressive statistics, he won't be getting his hands on the Liga trophy, which this season goes to Atlético Madrid. Real have to make do with the Copa del Rey, which they win on 16 April 2014 at the Mestalla, in Valencia, 3–0 against Barcelona. It's a match in which Cristiano doesn't play due to various injuries that have been plaguing him. Ever since the beginning of April, Cristiano's body has begun to give him warning signs. The doctors who examined him diagnosed tendinitis in the left knee and serious muscle inflammation. They recommended complete rest because they feared the problems could worsen. They said his body was on the edge. For the first time in his career, his seemingly indestructible chassis is failing him. But he doesn't pay much attention to the doctors, as he is determined to play in the Champions League final in Lisbon against Atlético. The effort proves to be worth the pain, as Real get to lift the trophy they have been dreaming about for years. It's their tenth Champions League title, and Cristiano's second.

It's a highly coveted prize, but there have been

other very special moments this season. A few days after Cristiano receives the 2013 Ballon d'Or, the President of Portugal, Cavaco Silva, names him a Grand Officer of the Order of Prince Henry (a Portuguese national order of knighthood), 'for his contribution to Portugal's international reach'.

2014–15 Season

After pushing his body to the max in recent months, Cristiano is plagued by fitness problems at the start of the new season. But it doesn't stop him playing in the European Super Cup against Sevilla on 12 August at Cardiff City Stadium, and scoring two goals to bag Real their first title of the season. A couple of weeks later, on 28 August, UEFA president Michel Platini presents him with the award for Best Player in Europe for the 2013–14 season. And the individual awards start piling up in the months that follow, from Best Player, Best Goal and Best Striker 2013–14 in Spain's Professional Football League, to Globe Soccer's Best Player of 2014.

It has been a golden year for Cristiano. He has ditched his individualistic style and has taken on more of a leadership role, despite not actually being captain. In the lead-up to Christmas he is unstoppable, scoring 25 goals between September and the end of 2014. And the team have time to squeeze in one more triumph just before the break, winning the Club World Cup in Morocco.

But at the beginning of 2015, just after the Ballon d'Or ceremony, everything shifts. It is a challenging time, both on and off the pitch. First, he splits up with long-term partner Irina Shayk. Then there is controversy surrounding his lavish 30th birthday celebrations on 7 February, just hours after the Whites' 4–0 thrashing by Atlético – their most humiliating defeat since Guardiola's Barça beat Real 5–0 under Mourinho back in November 2010. On this occasion, Ronaldo manages only one shot on target. 'We need to forget about this match as quickly as possible,' he concedes. It will prove to be a terrible season for Real, devoid of any Liga, Champions League or Copa del Rey trophies. Ronaldo has to console himself with being the top Liga goalscorer of the season and reaching his 300th goal for Real Madrid. Plus in April he nets five in a match for the first time in the team's 9–1 annihilation of Granada.

Meanwhile Messi's season has been more or less the reverse of Cristiano's. The first half is an ordeal, as he struggles to see eye to eye with new coach Luis Enrique, and the two end up in a feud. Messi is no longer untouchable, although it might be difficult to accept, and he tries his best to resist it, as happens on 20 October 2014 when he refuses to come off the pitch to be substituted during a match against Eibar. It seems the new coach has overlooked the comments of Pep Guardiola, who managed Barcelona from 2008 to 2012. 'Coaching Barça involves turning up at the training ground, calling Messi over, asking how he is, and then building the rest around that,' he once said.

But despite the tensions at the Nou Camp, Messi continues to outdo himself throughout the season. His greatest moment is on 22 November, when he becomes the top scorer in the history of La Liga with 253 goals, toppling the record of 251 set by Telmo Zarra some 60 years earlier. Leo dedicates this special achievement to his son Thiago, as well as his friend and former teammate Ronaldinho, who was instrumental in helping him settle at Barça. Three days later he overtakes Raúl González as the highest ever Champions League scorer.

And from January onwards the team's luck changes for the better. They are motivated by the 'Anoeta debacle', in which they are particularly humiliated during a 1–0 defeat by Real Sociedad. It's a rare match that sees Lionel start on the bench following a decision (or punishment, as some allege) by the technical staff. From that moment onwards, Leo and Luis Enrique reach an agreement to leave it all out on the pitch. And Barça's 'MSN' (Messi-Suárez-Neymar) trident transforms into a formidable strike force. 'We have a great relationship, and when there's an understanding off the pitch then it's much easier to play well together on the pitch,' explains the Flea.

The result: Barcelona's star is on the rise once again, winning La Liga and the Copa del Rey in May, and the Champions League on 6 June. It's the *Blaugrana*'s second treble in five years. It has been a much more fruitful year for Lionel, in radical contrast to the previous year. 'I feel happy. I admit that I started the season in a different place, after what happened to me last year. It was a difficult year with everything that happened off the pitch, as well as all my injuries and my performance. But this year I started again and I feel great.'

2015–16 Season

Barely six months after uttering these words, Leo finishes 2015 in the best possible way: with the Club World Cup in Japan. 'It's a wonderful tournament, one of my favourites. For its own sake but also because of what it represents: having won the Champions League. That year that we won everything under Guardiola seemed impossible to replicate, we really didn't know if we would be able to do it again one day. But here we are,' says the Argentine in an interview with Fifa.com just before the final against River Plate on 20 December. It's the second time in his career that he's up against an Argentine club – the previous time was against Estudiantes in the 2009 Club World Cup final. 'River is a great team at a world class level, I think it's going to be a good match.' And of course, not only does the Rosarino not disappoint, he leads his team to victory. He gets them off the mark in the 36th minute with a shot from the outside of his left boot following a headed pass by Neymar. The next two goals are scored by Suárez in the second half. It's 3–0 and Leo's Barça are the most successful club in the history of the tournament.

It's another triumph which banishes the memories of a tough start to the season – when an injury kept Leo off the pitch for nearly two months – and hints that the second half of the season will be as exceptional as the previous one. At the start of 2016 anything seems possible. The team is united, and any lack of understanding with the coach, which last year seemed on the verge of ruining the season, is a thing of the past. 'It was a bit difficult at the beginning, but once we did what we wanted to do, what the coach wanted, then from there we gradually began to improve and perform better and better,' explains Lionel.

La Liga seems to be all sewn up when Barcelona host Celta Vigo on 14 February. Leo doesn't know it yet, but it's going to be the most talked-about match of the season, and not just because of the stunning scoreline (6–1). He scores the first goal just before the half hour with a play from a dead ball, then helps Luis Suárez make it 2–1, and then has a hand in the third as well. And after impressing half the world by that point, he wows the other half by scoring the fourth in the 80th minute. He forces a penalty, places the ball on the penalty spot, and then, just when he is about to shoot, he stops short, allowing Suárez to swoop in from behind.

It's a move reminiscent of Ajax's Johan Cruyff and Jesper Olsen in 1982. Some hail it as masterful, while others think it shows a lack of respect. Leo stays out of the debate. All his attention is focused on one thing: winning La Liga.

As the season progresses, Leo chalks up another two records, becoming the first player to score 300 La Liga goals, and then, on 20 April, netting his 500th professional goal. Most of them have been scored with his left foot (more than 81 per cent). Twenty-five were from direct free kicks, 64 were penalties, and 411 were during open play. Four hundred and fifty have been for Barça, the rest with the Argentine national team. The latest personal achievement comes at the Riazor stadium against Deportivo de La Coruña, in a match that ends 0–8.

But despite the new milestones on his résumé, the final few weeks of the season are tougher than anticipated. Barça are knocked out of the Champions Leauge in the quarter-finals by Atlético Madrid, and Real are hot on their heels in La Liga. 'We had the advantage but then we took a hit. It was at a moment when we least expected it – right after the international break. Real Madrid crept up on us, we were knocked out by Atlético Madrid, there were all those Liga games where we lost lots of points … Fortunately we still believe in ourselves,' says Leo, in an attempt to calm the Barça fans. In fact, Real and Atlético don't just have to win, they need FC Barcelona to slip up. But the *Blaugrana* manage not to bow to the pressure, and on 14 May 2016 they beat Granada 0–3 in the final match of the competition. The Flea has succeeded in winning his eighth Liga in eleven seasons. One week later they lift the Copa del Rey after beating Sevilla 2–0.

And what about the Champions League? This time it belongs to Cristiano Ronaldo. The Portuguese will remember this season as the one in which he won his third European cup. 'I had a vision. I knew I was going to score the winning goal, and I said to Zizou, "Leave me till last in the penalty shootout because I'm going to score the winning penalty." And that's exactly what happened.' It's classic CR7 – no room for bashfulness as the Portuguese analyses what happened in the final against Atlético Madrid in Milan on 28 May. It's decided in the Russian Roulette of the penalty shoot-out, but he's the last one to step up, and his goal is worth the Champions League trophy. 'You're the best,' Zinedine Zidane is heard telling him during the celebrations on the pitch at the San Siro. And he is, at least in terms of the number of goals scored in the tournament. CR7 is the top scorer with a total of sixteen, nearly double that of Bayern Munich striker Robert Lewandowski, who is second with nine. Barça's Luis Suárez has snatched the La Liga top scorer and Golden Shoe awards from Cristiano this year, but when it comes to the Champions League no one comes close.

And as far as he's concerned, this is the one that counts. 'Barça's Liga and Copa del Rey "double" doesn't bother me, because I know that if we win the Champions League it's worth much more than the double. There are many star players who have never even won it once. Winning the Champions League is a dream. I'm telling you from the heart, I wouldn't switch it for anything,' he insists just a few days before the final.

With their triumph in Milan, Real manage to salvage one of the most turbulent seasons in the Whites' dugout in recent memory – including even under Mourinho's tenure. The season started with Rafa Benítez stepping in to replace Carlo Ancelotti, and it quickly became apparent that there was no chemistry between the new coach and the team's star player. The tension eventually forced the coach's departure and the subsequent arrival of Zinedine Zidane just after the Christmas break. From then on the team makes an unexpected comeback, culminating in the final in Milan and with Ronaldo becoming Real Madrid's top La Liga scorer with 231, as well as their highest ever scorer across all competitions: 324 in 308 matches – an average of 1.05 per game. One more goal and 433 fewer matches than previous record holder Raúl.

2016–17 Season

On 17 August 2016, having spent his whole career with the *Blaugrana*, Messi finally wins his first title as team captain. It's the Spanish Super Cup, which Barça take home after trouncing Sevilla 5–0 on aggregate, with two assists and one goal for the Argentine.

But the joyous start to the season does not continue into La Liga. A surprise defeat by Alavés on 10 September sets alarm bells ringing in the Barça camp, and when Messi is injured on 21 September at the Nou Camp, panic ensues. They are playing the second half against Atlético Madrid when Messi puts his hand to his waist and falls to the ground in the 58th minute, glancing over at the dugout, crestfallen. The tests clearly show he has torn a muscle in his right thigh. He'll be out for three weeks. It's not the first time this sort of injury has forced Leo out. He missed a month previously due to similar problems in his left leg while playing with Argentina – although the national team were quick to point the finger at the club. 'Barcelona are always sending us messages telling us to look after Messi, but they don't take care of him themselves,' national team coach Edgardo Bauza told Fox Sports.

With Neymar and Suárez at the helm, Barça manage to cope with the number 10's absence, and before long he returns with a bang: four consecutive victories in November, and two records – 500 goals for the club across professional matches and friendlies, and 100 in international competitions. But he unexpectedly falters on the day when all eyes are on him, during the

Clásico against Real Madrid. A goal from Sergio Ramos just before the final whistle gives the Whites a deserved 1–1 draw at the Nou Camp, and Barça's biggest rivals retain their La Liga lead after their toughest away game of the year.

Meanwhile, Ronaldo is gifted his first title of the season while recovering from a Euro 2016 injury, watching as his teammates crush Sevilla at the Lerkendal Stadion in Trondheim, Norway on 9 August in the European Super Cup. It finishes 3–2 after extra time, the best possible start to the season for the Whites. Ronaldo is ready to make his mark when Madrid's next shot at silverware presents itself in December, in the form of the Club World Cup in Japan. Top goal-scorer and player of the tournament, CR7 stands out thanks to his hat-trick in the final against Kashima Antlers, helping Real finish 2016 on a high by lifting the trophy.

Back in Madrid, they soon get a rare taste of disappointment. After an unbeaten run of 40 matches, they stumble on 15 January 2017 against Sevilla in La Liga, and then again in the Copa del Rey against Celta Vigo. After a shock 2–1 victory for Celta at the Bernabéu and a 2–2 draw in the return leg, the underdogs manage to knock Zidane's men out of a competition for the first time this season, and Ronaldo has to endure the fans' whistling and jeering in Real's subsequent matches.

Leo and Cristiano will not come face to face in the Copa del Rey again until 2018, but before that they meet again in the Champions League, where the *Blaugrana* secure a historic victory before falling from grace. In the return leg of the final sixteen, after losing 4–0 against Paris St Germain at the Parc des Princes on 14 February, Luis Enrique's men pull off the greatest comeback in the history of the competition, sealing a 6–1 victory (6–5 on aggregate) in the dying moments. Messi only scores once, from the penalty spot, but he is the star in an iconic photo, the most memorable image of the night. It is taken by freelance Mexican photographer Santiago Garcés who works with the club, and shows the Rosarino, right fist raised, standing high on one of the barriers at the edge of the pitch, surrounded by a sea of fans. It's a perfect portrait of celebration, reflecting the delirium of the fans at the climactic moment, as well as Messi's leadership. It immediately becomes the clubs most popular Instagram post, with 1.6 million likes in 36 hours. It garners 2.6 million likes on Facebook and 56 million views, as well as 2.5 million views on Twitter.

Unfortunately, Juventus destroy their Champions League hopes just a few weeks later in the quarter-final (3–0 in the first leg, 0–0 in the return), and Leo and his teammates kiss the trophy goodbye, just before another trip to the Bernabéu to continue their battle for La Liga. Real and Barça are separated by two points and Real have a game in hand. The finale is a breathless affair. Real manage to equalise to make it 2–2 in the

85th minute, but it is Messi who dominates the front pages the next day with a sensational winner in the 90th from the edge of the area. It's his 500th official goal for Barça, in an unparalleled moment which deserves a special celebration. After hugging his teammates, he takes off his shirt at the corner, turning it round to show the number 10 to the fans. He stands there for a few seconds, looking serious, then makes the sign of the cross, opens his arms and looks to the sky, before returning to the centre of the pitch with the rest of the team. That night, with one extra match played, Barça are top of La Liga.

Neither team then puts a foot wrong, so thanks to their match in hand Real are crowned champions of La Liga on 21 May in Málaga. Cristiano is perhaps the least happy member of the team, weighed down by the criticism he has endured throughout the season. 'They talk about me as if I'm a delinquent. When people talk about Cristiano, they get it wrong, both on and off the pitch,' he says in the press area afterwards. 'I'm not a saint, but nor am I the devil that a lot of people make me out to be.'

A week later, the final of the Copa del Rey against Deportivo Alavés represents Messi and Barça's last chance of the season to win a trophy. In the 29th minute, some great passing between Messi and Neymar allows the Argentine to open the scoring. It's a beautiful shot by the Flea from the edge of the area, and goalkeeper Pacheco can't do anything to stop it. Before his teammates have even arrived to congratulate him, half the world's football analysts are busy telling their radio, TV and online audiences a crucial stat: Barcelona have never lost a final when Messi has scored.

And this one is no exception, despite Alavés equalising shortly afterwards with an incredible Theo Hernández free kick. Neymar restores the *Blaugrana*'s lead in the 44th minute, assisted by André Gomes, and immediately after that a stunning trick by Messi seals the deal. Hemmed in by four opponents with almost no way of getting to the edge of the area, the little magician slaloms between them before flicking a perfect through ball to Alcácer, who makes it 3–1 with a low shot across goal.

Messi has amassed 30 titles with Barcelona and it's the eighth consecutive season in which he has scored more than 40 goals. Another record, as is the fact that during the same period he has always scored at least 25 goals in each competition. He claims the Pichichi top goalscorer award for the fourth time, along with his fourth Golden Shoe. As if that wasn't enough, Dutch magazine *Voetbal* names him the best player in history, ahead of Maradona, Cruyff, Pelé and Di Stéfano, while rival Cristiano Ronaldo doesn't even make it into the top five.

Nonetheless, during a promotional trip to China, Leo admits on ESPN Asia: 'We would have liked to have made it to the Champions League final and won La Liga. It wasn't to be this year, we tried but it wasn't going to happen. We have the Copa del Rey and we hope that next year will be a better one for us in terms of titles.'

Meanwhile, Ronaldo is on his way to the Champions League final in Cardiff, after playing a decisive role in the quarters against Bayern Munich, scoring three times (becoming the first player to score 100 goals in the competition) and in the semis with another hat-trick in the first leg against Atlético Madrid. 'Cristiano, king of the Champions,' declares *Marca* the next morning. 'Cristiano Ronaldo is now CR9, the best striker in the world,' writes *La Gazzetta dello Sport*. 'He's the favourite to retain his Ballon d'Or title, now more than ever,' predicts *L'Équipe*.

And the man himself is aware of his vital role. 'Too much humility is no good. We need to let our abilities shine through, show them who's best.' His comments at Real Madrid's Open Media Day before the final show that he is hungry for victory. And his confidence bears fruit in the 20th minute, as fans watch him linking up neatly with Carvajal, before sweeping the ball low into the net, helped by a deflection from Bonucci. Juve aren't ready to give up, equalising with a stunning volley from Mandžukić before the half hour mark. But the Whites give them no time to relax. They are focused and the Juventus resistance cracks in the second half, with Real running out 4–1 winners.

On the edge of the pitch, Man of the Match Ronaldo tells broadcaster Antena 3: 'I was fully prepared for this, because the finals are always the most important matches. It was a great opportunity for me, and for my coach, and I'm very happy.' Aside from team trophies, Ronaldo has excelled on an individual level. He has scored the most goals in the Champions League in the season, reached 400 goals for Real Madrid and become the top goal-scorer of all time across the five biggest European leagues with 371, overtaking Jimmy Greaves record of 366 set in 1971. If 2016 was incredible, the first half of 2017 has been even better.

* * *

The comparison over several seasons gives some idea of these two players' incredible achievements. It is also worth looking at how many titles they have each won with their clubs. Leo is in the lead by far, as he has benefited from some of Barça's best years (or is it the other way around?). He has won eight La Liga trophies, seven Spanish Super Cups, four Champions Leagues, five Copas del Rey, three UEFA Super Cups and three Club World Cups – all with Barcelona. Cristiano Ronaldo dos Santos Aveiro cannot quite match Messi in terms of trophies. He has won 22 titles with his three clubs – Sporting Lisbon, Manchester United and Real. Four Champions Leagues, three Club World Cups, one FA Cup, two League Cups, two Community Shields, three Premier League titles, two La Liga trophies, two Copas del Rey, two UEFA Super Cups and one Spanish Super Cup.

It's 30–22 to the Argentine.

Chapter 4

Argentina versus Portugal

Cristiano and Leo debut with their home nations' first teams at the tender age of eighteen. For CR7 it's a match to remember, whereas it's definitely one to forget as far as Leo is concerned.

Ronaldo hears about his call-up to the first team via a phone call from his mother Dolores. Shortly afterwards, his agent Jorge Mendes confirms the good news that he will be included for a friendly against Kazakhstan on 14 August 2003. 'I am happy and proud to be one of the chosen ones,' says Ronaldo. 'I am very grateful to the selectors. This is a very special moment in my life, all the good things have come at once – first the transfer to Man United and now the national team. I want to play and I want to win.' On 20 August 2003 in Chaves, Portugal, Ronaldo dons the red and green shirt for the first time. Coach Luiz Felipe Scolari brings him on in the second half, replacing Luís Figo. He suddenly finds himself surrounded by the champions he has always looked up to as role models. His mentors Luís Figo and Rui Costa have told him to stay calm and play the way he always does. Above all, they tell him not to let his emotions get the better of him. The youngster follows their advice to the letter and the press later name him man of the match.

Messi's first outing with the Argentine first team is two years later, on 17 August 2005. It's also in a friendly, in this case against Hungary in Budapest at the Ferenc Puskás Stadium. But unlike with Cristiano, his debut is a fiasco – and he is only on the pitch for 40 seconds. He comes on for Maxi López in the 65th minute. On his second touch, he dribbles the ball past Vanczák. The Hungarian grabs him by his brand-new number 18 shirt; Messi lifts his arm and pushes him back. Bam! He catches the defender full in the face. German referee Markus Merk is in no doubt. He elbowed him. And he pulls out the red card in front of the disbelieving Argentina players. Sent off in his first match. Not the scenario that Leo had imagined. He spends the rest of the match crying. His coach and teammates think the referee's decision is excessive, but their words of consolation are in vain.

No one could have predicted such a catastrophic start when, barely a year earlier, Argentine Football Association (AFA) youth coach Hugo Tocalli had first heard promising things about Lionel. 'They brought me a videotape of a boy who was playing in Barcelona. I really liked what he could do, but … in those sorts of cases I'm always worried that the tape is from some footballing agent. Besides, the kid was very young … So I said to myself, no … I'll wait a while. I go off to Finland with the Under-17s and when I get back I find out more about this player. Everyone has told me great things about him. I go and see Grondona (Julio Grondona, then AFA president, who passed away in 2014), and I schedule an opportunity to see the kid in two friendlies, against Paraguay and Uruguay.'

Everything is agreed: they organise two friendlies to see this kid who is currently making waves in Europe. The first request sent to Barcelona has his name spelt incorrectly, asking for them to spare 'Leonel Mecci' some time to come over to Argentina; the request is politely rejected. He has Copa del Rey commitments. But the AFA are in a hurry to see him play, so they send another request. Leo has lived in Spain for three years, he plays in the Barça youth leagues, and there is a risk of losing him and seeing him in a Furia Roja shirt (Red Fury, as the Spanish national shirt is nicknamed). It is not such a remote possibility, given that only a year earlier during the Copa de España in Albacete, Under-16 coach Ginés Menéndez had offered Leo the chance to play for Spain. 'No thank you' was the reply he received. Despite living on the Iberian peninsula, Leo feels deeply Argentine. But who knows, perhaps after some insistence, the kid might change his mind? Either way, the AFA feel it is better to pre-empt the Spanish Football Federation.

The match against Paraguay is on 29 June 2004. Leo is not starting, partly because of his age, partly out of respect to the team, and also because they do not want to put too much pressure on him. In the second half, in the 50th minute, when Argentina are already winning 3–0, Tocalli approaches him. He puts a hand on his shoulder and says to him: 'Go with the trainer, who is heading down to the pitch.' Surprised and excited, the Flea bursts on to the pitch wearing the Albiceleste (sky-blue-and-white) shirt for the first time. And he shows what he can do: he picks off his opponents and scores a goal.

'You could see it in the way he played,' says Tocalli. 'If he was good in training, on the pitch he was something else.' The friendly ends 8–0 and the youngster has seriously impressed the coaches. So much so that, that very night, Tocalli receives a call from his friend and youth coach predecessor, José Pékerman. 'He asked me where I had found the boy. He thought he was fantastic. "You're going to start him in the next match against Uruguay, right?" he asked me.' But no. In the match against Uruguay, in Colonia, Leo is not in the starting line-up. When he comes on, however, he surprises everyone again. The next day, Sunday 4 July, the Buenos Aires sports magazine *Olé* writes: 'Young Messi is the real deal. He scored two goals, made four assists, and was the one to watch in the 4–1 victory over Uruguay.'

Leo's double trial has been a definitive success. He

has really impressed them. And now Tocalli has no doubts about including him in the squad for the South American Youth Championship (a qualifying tournament for the FIFA Under-20 World Cup) the following January. The tournament takes place in Colombia, at high altitude, and the Argentines don't find it particularly easy to adapt. Apart from in three matches, Leo only ever goes onto the pitch in the second half. 'That was my decision,' says Tocalli, justifying himself. 'The boy still hadn't got into the rhythm of the entire team, he was used to playing in the Barça youth leagues, he didn't have the same intensity that's needed to play in South America … they were very demanding matches. And to add to that his opponents were from the '85 leagues, and two years make a big difference at that age. So I decided to use him with caution so as not to tire him out or give him too much responsibility.'

It's a tactic that pays dividends. Messi scores five goals and finishes as the second-highest scorer in the competition. Argentina come third behind Colombia and Brazil, meaning they qualify for the Under-20 World Cup, to be held in the Netherlands. The competition kicks off on Saturday 11 June 2005, and Argentina's first test is against the United States. To the fans' surprise, the Flea is not in the starting line-up, and the Albiceleste lose 1–0.

It's a bad start to the tournament but Leo keeps everybody calm: 'I'm in a very good state of mind and

I think I'm up to playing for 90 minutes, but I have to respect the coach's decisions.' He adds: 'The team will pick up the pace because we have some good players. We have everything we need to qualify.' He is spot on and they prove it on 14 June against Egypt. This time he is in the starting line-up. He scores the first goal, weakening the Africans' resolve, leaving Zabaleta to seal the scoreline definitively. The third match, against Germany, is a tricky one: it will decide who goes into the last sixteen. The Germans have one point more than the Argentines, so a draw will suffice for them to go through. But Messi makes his mark. He gets the ball in the middle of the pitch, slaloms past the defenders and makes a precise pass. Oberman lets the ball go past him and Neri Cardoso scores to make it 1–0. Next up they beat Colombia 2–1, followed by Spain, 3–1.

In the semis they face Brazil in a hotly anticipated duel between two teams who have each won the tournament four times. Within eight minutes the Albiceleste are already dominating, thanks to a torpedo-like shot from Messi from outside the area, which just edges in at the goalpost, rendering the Brazilian goalie's spectacular dive completely futile. Renato equalises in the second half, but in the last minute, after Leo gets past his opponent for the umpteenth time, Zabaleta picks up a rebound off a Brazilian defender and manages to score. And then comes the final, at 8.00pm on 2 July at the Galgenwaard Stadium in Utrecht. The opposition are

Nigeria, who have beaten Morocco in the semi-finals. The previous day, a Dutch TV channel had presented Messi with a golden clog, the trophy that declares him player of the tournament. 'I'm very happy and I thank you for this prize,' he says. 'The truth is that I'm very surprised at everything that has happened to me here.'

And the surprises continue into the final. In the 38th minute, Messi controls the ball down the left-hand touchline. He begins a 45-yard zigzagging run and gets into the box. Dele Adeleye realises that he cannot snatch the ball from him and instead knocks him down. There is no doubt in referee Terje Hauge's mind: it's a penalty. Leo takes it without a run-up, softly, with his left foot, to the right of Vanzekin, who throws himself in exactly the opposite direction: 1–0. In the 52nd minute Chinedu Ogbuke levels the scores for Nigeria. In the 73rd minute Argentina's Agüero is fouled by Monday James in front of goal. Leo steps up to the spot once more and shoots with precision into the left-hand side of the goal: 2–1. Argentina win their fifth Under-20 title. Leo Messi is the star player.

He might be a star but he is still extremely shy. In the dressing room he stays in his corner and barely says a word or interacts with his teammates. But to be fair, although it's hard to imagine it now, at that time Leo is virtually unknown on the other side of the Atlantic. He's effectively a foreigner, having grown up far from his native country. 'He was a very shy kid, he didn't know anyone and no one knew him,' recalls Tocalli. His demeanour only shifts during training sessions or when he's playing. And it's much the same story when he eventually reaches the first team, because the biggest challenge has not been adapting to Argentine football – which is very different in style to the European game – but rather finding his place in a close-knit team with well-established relationships.

It's a problem Cristiano has never encountered with Portugal. He is playing with the national team in June 2003 at the Festival International Espoirs de Toulon et du Var (the 'Toulon Hopefuls Tournament' as it is known) when he catches the attention of the scouts who attend the competition year after year. It began in 1967 as an Under-21 club tournament and in 1974 it switched to national teams only. It is not recognised by FIFA, but it has long been considered a place for talent-spotting the youngsters who years later are confirmed as global superstars.

Although the Madeiran doesn't win the prize for best player (which goes to Argentina's Javier Mascherano), the Portugal team triumph for the third time, following their victories in 1992 and 2001. More importantly, Cristiano makes a good impression. 'I have done what I came here to do,' he says. 'In three of the fixtures I think I played well but in the other two I was a bit tired. It's not surprising when you consider how many games are squeezed into such a short space of time.'

In each of the national teams, CR7 always plays alongside slightly older teammates. He is fourteen when he joins the Under-15s and sixteen when he goes to the Under-17s. He is eighteen in the Under-20s team in Toulon, where he makes an impression right from the start during the first match against England in Nîmes on 11 June. 'He is an extremely interesting player,' comments seasoned Barcelona scout Joan Martínez Vilaseca. 'He has unique characteristics that make him a promising young man. If he stays focused on his career, one day he will be able to play for one of the big European clubs if he puts his mind to it. It won't be long before he's one of the best players in Portugal, no doubt about it.' It is an understatement given the turn the player's career is about to take.

But how does the eighteen-year-old feel given his performance at Toulon and the slew of clubs now taking an interest in him? 'I don't feel pressured by it all,' he replies. 'I am just excited and happy to know that the big clubs and the top names have noticed me. It gives me strength and encouragement to try to improve every day. But I haven't spoken to anyone yet, and no one has made a concrete offer to Sporting. I know there's a lot of talk in the press, but right now my main objective is to get the team to the final and help them win. That's what I have to focus on.'

And he does. Although he doesn't score in the final against Italy, he plays well and helps Portugal to a 3–1 victory. The players are treated to a heroes' welcome and a big celebration back in Lisbon, but Cristiano is not with them. He has stayed in France for a few days with his mother and one of his sisters to take a break before his life changes forever on 6 August. Man United have been taking their time over him, but the French tournament has now accelerated the transfer process.

That summer, Ronaldo bids farewell to Sporting to become a Premier League star. A year later, he plays in his first big competition with the senior Portugal team, UEFA Euro 2004 in his home country, which ends with CR7 in tears on the pitch after losing the final to Greece. But at least he has now cemented his position in Scolari's team, at just nineteen years of age. After coming on as a substitute during the first two matches, he is in the starting line-up in every subsequent match.

Two summers later in Germany he gets to experience his first World Cup. Along with Messi, the fans include him on the shortlist of six players who are nominated for best young player of the tournament. Once again it all ends in tears, as France knock Portugal out in the semi-finals thanks to a Zinedine Zidane penalty. France are headed for the final against Italy in Berlin – the final of Zidane's headbutt against Materazzi and a fourth World Cup win for Italy. On 8 July 2006, Portugal are defeated 3–1 by Germany in the race for third place at the Gottlieb-Daimler-Stadion in Stuttgart.

Germany 2006 is also Messi's first World Cup. All of

Argentina wants to see him in the starting line-up and they have pinned all their hopes on him. They want to see proof of all the amazing stories that are told across Europe about the heir to Maradona – and they want to see that proof in the national shirt. Since the days of the *Pibe de Oro* ('Golden Boy' – Maradona's nickname) they have dreamt of having another player, a spectacular, magical player, whom they can love and worship the way they did Diego (and still do). The Flea watches the first match against the Ivory Coast from the bench, after coach José Pékerman exercises caution over his age, as well as over a recent injury which is still causing some niggles.

He will have to wait until 16 June to go on to the pitch, when Argentina face Serbia and Montenegro. He comes on in the second half for Maxi Rodríguez, and thirteen minutes later becomes the youngest player to score in an Albiceleste shirt, netting the team's sixth goal in the tournament. He is eighteen years, eleven months and 23 days old. It has been a much better debut than his earlier friendly when he was sent off, but it's not enough to earn a place in the starting line-up. In fact, he doesn't even play a single minute of the quarter-final against Germany, which ends with Argentina being knocked out 4–2 on penalties, following a last-gasp equaliser to make it 1–1 at the end of extra time. 'I am proud of him and I was the one who included him in the Under-20 team when no one knew who he was,'

Pékerman will later say. 'In Argentina the problem is that we have so much faith that just a little bit of Messi gets us very excitable. And people were expecting Messi to be the great Maradona of this World Cup. And he was just taking his first steps with Argentina, a great team. I hope this experience will serve him well in the future.'

Four years later in South Africa, Maradona himself has taken the reins of the Albiceleste, and things are a little bit different. The coach has a soft spot for his heir apparent, and on the eve of the tournament he explains: 'I think he is the best in the world. And he's Argentine. I've already told the boys: "If Leo gets the ball, we'll have plenty of chances." I'm trying to get it into their heads that they're a team. And that we need Messi to play the way he does at Barça. Messi knows that his teammates want him to be the cherry on the cake. He needs to lead them. We don't want him there as a soloist – not in training and not on the pitch. When we're playing, they can't pass it to me anymore … so if they don't pass it to Messi, then we're getting it wrong.'

And the deluge of compliments will continue following their opening match on Saturday 12 June 2010 against Nigeria. Leo is the best in Argentina. He lights up the Albiceleste's game, he understands the needs of the team and he is the most active member of the Argentine attack. At the end of the match, won by a header from Gabriel Heinze, Maradona rushes over to Messi and lifts him up in his arms. It seems Leo might finally have found his place in the national team, and won over the fans who don't like the fact that he has never played for a first division Argentine club. He even gets to wear the captain's armband in the final group stage match against Greece, something he has been dreaming of for a long time. Argentina win a tough match 2–0 and are through to the last sixteen with three group stage victories. When the press ask him about the possible 'Messidependence' of the Argentine team, Leo replies: 'This team doesn't depend on me. On the contrary, I'm the one who depends on the midfielders getting me the ball.'

Just three days after he celebrates his 23rd birthday, Argentina dispatch their Mexican rivals 3–1 in the last sixteen. It is not an easy game for Lionel. He looks uncomfortable and he doesn't get on the scoresheet. It once again sparks debate about the number 10's position, the midfielders, and Maradona's choice of formation. And against Germany in the quarters, Maradona's tactical gambles fail Messi again and again, just when it matters most. It is fifteen minutes before he even touches the ball. He tries to organise and direct the play, but apart from a few runs which go nowhere, the odd tackle, and a couple of misguided shots, there is very little of note. He is left in no man's land, foundering fast. His World Cup scoring record is dismal. He has played five matches, he has taken more shots than anyone – 30, with twelve on target and two off the post

– but he has had no luck. After the match, Maradona calls it 'the hardest moment in my life, a real blow'. But Messi says nothing, he can only shed tears.

Meanwhile, Cristiano is having a similarly disappointing experience. He arrives in South Africa not having scored with Portugal for fifteen months, but initially he is bursting with anticipation. 'I want to play well, I want to be the best in the tournament. I'm not saying I'll necessarily be the top goal-scorer or anything like that, but I'm going to give it my all and try and be the best. It's always my aim to be the best, but we'll see. I really want to do well in this World Cup and I believe I can succeed. But when I say that I want to play well, have a good tournament and help my team win, that doesn't mean to say I have to prove myself to anyone.'

Portugal make it through the group stages unbeaten and the only team of the 32 World Cup finalists yet to concede a goal. They face Spain in the last sixteen. Portugal vs Spain is always a special match because of the neighbourly rivalry – be it historic, cultural, social or sporting. Plus the two teams have never played each other in a World Cup. And let's not forget the Cristiano factor. The number 7 has terrorised the Spanish defenders in La Liga, and now he will come face to face with the likes of teammates Sergio Ramos and Íker Casillas. And not only has he returned to goal-scoring form with Portugal, he has been voted the best player in the team's group stage matches. As Casillas says: 'When a player like him is inspired, it's almost impossible to stop him.'

But as the national anthems play at the Green Point Stadium in Cape Town on 29 June, Cristiano remains silent. It's a bad sign, almost a premonition of how the match will pan out for him. It's a disaster: only four shots, two on target. The only moment worth mentioning is when he crosses with a *rabona*, a speciality of his, where one leg crosses behind the other to kick the ball, avoiding having to turn. That's about it in terms of his performance. After David Villa's goal for Spain in the 67th minute, Cristiano is seen standing alone, hands on hips, looking over at the dugout, as if demanding an explanation, pleading for some help and advice in order to turn their fortunes around. After the final whistle, he walks away from his defeated and broken team, booed by the Spanish fans, and even some of the Portuguese. The camera follows him closely as he heads for the dressing room, his face expressionless. Suddenly he turns and spits – it's unclear whether it's directed at the cameraman or the ground. Either way it's an ugly gesture and the press pounce on it, criticising the Real player's behaviour. Cristiano is in the eye of the storm. Everyone in Portugal wants to know why he doesn't play like he plays with Real when he is with the national team. It's a feeling Lionel Messi knows all too well, the helplessness at not being able to explain the unexplainable.

Two years later at Euro 2012 in Poland and Ukraine, he makes it up to the fans. On 27 June Portugal are knocked out in the semis, again by Spain, but this time the reception back home is much more positive. His performance and attitude throughout the tournament have been different. And no one back home has any lingering doubts. Cristiano is the best in the world. It hardly matters that in the following World Cup in Brazil in 2014, the team are knocked out in the group stages for the first time since 2002 and CR7 only manages to score a single goal. To be fair, it has been tough for him physically following a long and busy season at Real Madrid. The press is full of the usual criticism, but this time the team stand united. 'We are leaving with our heads held high. We tried to do our best but football is like this,' insists Cristiano following the elimination. He has played in three World Cups, and for the third time his dreams have been out of reach. He has played 1,114 minutes, thirteen matches, and scored three goals. At least he can console himself with the title of top scorer in Portugal's history, with 61. By the time of the next World Cup, Russia 2018, he will be 33. Who knows …

Leo Messi already has his sights set on Russia 2018 as Brazil 2014 ends in disappointment for him as well, with an excruciating final against Germany. But like Cristiano, he is his country's top scorer of all time with a total of 55 goals, after overtaking the record set by

Gabriel Batistuta, who played with the Argentine team from 1991 to 2002. Plus he has an Olympic gold medal to his name after the Albiceleste beat Nigeria in Beijing in 2008 thanks to a solitary goal by Ángel Di María. The most talked about match of those Olympic Games was their semi-final against Brazil, which will go down in history for the way the Albiceleste crushed and humiliated the Canaries, beating them 3–0. It's a clash that confirms the turning of the tide: Ronaldinho's time at the top is coming to an end, while Messi's ascent is unstoppable. At the end of the match, Ronnie – his friend, mentor and ex-Barça teammate – finds solace in the arms of his 'little brother' Messi. It's the photo that appears in all the papers the following day, a snapshot that shows just how cruel the world of sport can be.

But it can also be wonderful. During summer 2016 Ronaldo experiences both extremes – not just in a single tournament, but in a single match. For the second time in its history the Portuguese national team has made it to the final of the Euros, on 10 July at the Parc des Princes. In a role reversal from the previous occasion, the Portuguese are facing the hosts, France, and this time they are victorious. Their overall performance throughout the tournament has been poor, with three draws in the group phase (against Austria, Hungary and Iceland) and only managing to seal one victory within 90 minutes throughout the entire tournament, in the semi-final against Wales. Despite everything, Cristiano has scored some excellent goals and claims the Silver Boot (with three goals and three assists) and finally gets his chance to win a trophy with the national team. But his presence on the pitch in Paris is fleeting: in the sixteenth minute he takes a knock to the knee after a rough tackle by Dimitri Payet, and falls to the ground, evidently in pain. Although he tries to continue, he is replaced by Quaresma in the 24th minute. The next hour and a half sees him cut an increasingly frustrated figure on the sidelines, attempting to shout instructions as if he were the coach before giving his teammates a pep talk in a huddle before extra time. The scoreline doesn't change until the 109th minute, when an Éder strike puts Portugal ahead. Cristiano celebrates what is to be the only goal of the match, half-running half-hopping along the touchline, before accepting the trophy just minutes later from Spanish Football Federation president Ángel María Villar. With the Portuguese flag tied around his waist, barely able to stand on his bad leg, Cristiano kisses the cup and shouts to the heavens before bursting into tears. This time, they are tears of joy.

Chapter 5

Duels

It's 27 May 2009. Cristiano is dressed in white, the Man United second strip. Messi is wearing Barça's traditional *blaugrana* (blue and claret) colours. One has just been named as the best player on the continent – although he has not had a particularly brilliant season – while the other's star is on the rise. It is a hotly anticipated duel, and it's the perfect match for it: a Champions League final between two of the best teams in football.

The two stars arrive at the Stadio Olimpico in Rome conscious of the weight on their shoulders. All eyes are on them, although they refuse to acknowledge it. 'Messi is a great player, but tomorrow it's about Barcelona and Manchester United,' says Cristiano the night before the match. Leo agrees, saying that to focus on an individual duel 'would be disrespectful to two great teams – the two teams who are currently playing the best football. Two teams who have many other players who can be decisive.' Regardless, Cristiano versus Messi dominates the discussion. Even Sir Alex Ferguson weighs in on it, although he can't decide: 'They're both fantastic players who can create and score goals, both of them. When great players get to that level, it's all about the small details. One of them could have an off-night on the night. Other than that, what can you say about such good players?'

For the Portuguese it's a chance to lift the trophy for the second year running. For the Argentine, it would feel like a first, because despite having been part of the team that won it in Paris back in 2006, he missed the final due to injury. But for the Italian press it's about more than just the title at hand, it's also indicative of who will win the next Ballon d'Or. 'Whoever wins this may well have a better chance,' concedes Ronaldo, 'but that's not important. What I really want is to win the Champions League.' It has not escaped anyone's notice that this is the perfect opportunity for the Flea to get ahead of his greatest rival, although he doesn't see it that way. 'The important thing is the prize at stake for the team. One thing for sure is that whoever wins in Rome will be heralded as the best team in Europe.'

Kick-off at the Stadio Olimpico is at 8.46pm. Man United put the pressure on, pushing forward into their opponents' half. Barça are struggling to find their feet. Ronaldo is exceptional – the driving force behind United's game. In contrast, Messi has yet to get into the game. His father, Jorge, sees it too: 'I saw that Leo was out of the game for quite a while, and only once we scored the goal I began to see him get more involved.' In fact, the Flea contributes little until nine minutes after Eto'o has put Barcelona in front in the tenth minute. He leaves the right-hand touchline, looks to move into the centre, and unleashes a cracking shot from 35 yards, which is just too high. In the 22nd minute Cristiano heads at goal, but it goes over the bar. It's the number 7's sixth chance so far, and he seems determined to win the match on his own if he has to.

But gradually Barcelona take control. Messi gets better and better, although it is not his best night and he only manages to penetrate the forest of white shirts a few times. Finally the smallest player on the pitch makes his mark in the 70th minute. Xavi recovers the ball after a deflection from the United defence. He approaches the box, looks up and unleashes a spinning cross, smooth and precise. With his back to the defenders, Messi ascends to the Roman heavens, leaping high into the air and heading the ball towards the post, just as the goalie dives the wrong way. It's 2–0. Eight minutes later, Ronaldo is looking tired and distracted. He has a disagreement with Rooney and, irritated, he gets himself a yellow card for a needless foul on Puyol when he had no way to reach the ball.

At the final whistle, Leo rushes over to jump on coach Guardiola. 'I feel like the happiest man in the world. It's like I'm dreaming; it's the most important victory of my life. I dedicate it to my family and to Argentina. This team deserves it after the great work they have put in all year,' he gushes.

Meanwhile Cristiano has missed out on the history-making win he wanted so badly. When he goes up to collect his medal from UEFA president Michel Platini, the hissing and booing is audible – the Barça fans already see him as a symbol of Real Madrid, as the Whites have been actively pursuing him. Later, in his suit, and still hurting, he will say: 'It wasn't a match between Messi and me, but his team was better than us, and he was too because he scored.' The defeated pays homage to the victor. Some time later he will acknowledge how difficult it was to accept that particular defeat: 'I was very fragile that night. I was on the verge of crying on the pitch in front of millions of TV viewers. I hate losing, especially in a final like that.' It's his last final in a Man United shirt. For Messi, it's the start of a golden era. The following day, the front-page headline in Rome sports paper *Corriere dello Sport* reads: 'Messi: King of Europe'.

The next time the Portuguese and the Argentine come face to face will be in La Liga in Spain. From the 2009–10 season onwards, their names will be practically inseparable, and the comparisons show no signs of abating. They have become the figureheads for the bigger historic duel between Real Madrid and FC Barcelona, and almost every encounter between the two escalates into a matter of national importance. So far they have competed in 25 *Clásicos*, and while Leo is winning on results (twelve victories to the Portuguese's seven), Cristiano is ahead on goals (sixteen to CR7, fifteen to the Flea).

Of all the duels, there is one in particular that is etched in the collective memory, not because of the two players' performances, neither of which is spectacular, but because of the scoreline: 5–0 to Barça. The match takes place on Monday 29 November 2010 at the Nou Camp. It is a strange day for a Barça–Real match, but there are general elections in Catalonia on the Sunday, so it is better not to compound the politics with added drama. Adverts about the game have hailed it as the most closely matched *Clásico* for years, indicating the possibility of a transfer of power from Barcelona to Real Madrid. Why? Because popular opinion has it that Cristiano is better than Messi, plus Mourinho – who is the Real coach at the time – is not Manuel Pellegrini, nor is he Bernd Schuster or Juande Ramos or even Fabio Capello.

The Portuguese coach is the one who successfully crushed the *Blaugrana*'s collective efforts from the Inter dugout just six months earlier, denying Guardiola and co. their ticket to the Champions League final in Madrid. He is the man chosen by the Real president as the antidote to the Catalan magic. A coach who, from the highest position in La Liga (unbeaten, and one point ahead of Barça), questions Barcelona's successes and accuses the referees and rival managers of handing them all the power.

Meanwhile, Cristiano limits himself to saying that the *Blaugrana* play more of a 'tiki-taka' game and the Whites play with the sole objective of scoring as quickly as possible. He says that Barcelona are still an extremely difficult team to beat, even if they haven't won six titles this year (as they did in the previous campaign). 'They are just as good as they have always been over the last few years, a very strong team, especially at home. They have demonstrated that they can give us a run for our money in La Liga.' He doesn't mention Lionel, preferring to emphasise how well Real Madrid have been doing: 'We know that we are in a good place. That's why it will be a good match. May the best team win at the Nou Camp. And the best team will be Real Madrid.'

Sadly, Cristiano loses his bet. On that Monday at the Nou Camp, Barça teach their visitors a lesson in majestic football, while the Whites have no idea how to respond to the back-and-forth style of play which leaves their formation in tatters. By the end of a cold and rainy night, the *Blaugrana* have five goals and it could have easily been six, seven or eight without anyone calling foul play. Real Madrid are drowning in cold, deep waters. Ronaldo has been almost invisible. He is forced to run against the current, waiting in the pouring rain for passes which never arrive. The only moments worth noting are a free kick from 45 yards which is just wide and a one-on-one with Valdés which goes nowhere. Other moments are noteworthy for the wrong reasons, after the tension of the match causes him to lose his nerve and get himself into trouble. After the ball goes out and lands near the home team's dugout, Guardiola recovers it, dummies a throw-in, and then drops it back on the ground ready for Cristiano, who has just arrived to pick up the ball and continue the game. The Portuguese responds by pushing the rival coach, who staggers backwards. Andrés Iniesta and Víctor Valdés intervene: cue insults and more pushing. To prevent the situation from getting out of control, referee Iturralde González quickly shows Cristiano the yellow card. The fans in the stands start to whistle at him. Nothing else remarkable happens.

Ronaldo has failed to score in a single one of the six matches he has played against Barça so far. But today Messi hasn't scored either. Indeed, he has never scored against a team managed by Mourinho, be it Chelsea, Inter or Real. This match breaks a run of ten consecutive games in which he has scored, but he is effective nonetheless; he is generous and helps set up goals three and four for David Villa with surgical precision. The Flea has ruffled Carvalho, Lass, Pepe and Sergio Ramos's composure, and after a senseless foul on the Argentine in the 92nd minute and a punch-up with Puyol and Ramos, the red card finally comes out. Ramos has lost control, which is not unusual in such a game of nerves, particularly when the Whites know that Mourinho's game plan is still under construction, his ideas still need fine tuning, and he still doesn't know how to beat his eternal rivals. Interestingly, this is the first time a team led by Mourinho has been beaten 5–0.

Messi and Ronaldo probably have fonder memories of their Liga clash on 7 October 2012, once again at the Nou Camp. CR7 had already scored twelve in the season so far, eight of them in the last four matches, including two hat-tricks: one against Ajax in the Champions League, and one against Deportivo de La Coruña in the Spanish championship. Leo had scored ten, but had not netted any in the last three matches. This time they are both on target, scoring two each, and leading a wonderfully intense and impassioned performance, which certainly doesn't disappoint the TV audience of 400 million spectators. 'Out of this world,' reads the headline in Spanish sports paper *Marca*, continuing: 'Messi and Cristiano unleash two goals apiece because they are the best in the world.'

And there are plenty of other moments worth recalling. The Portuguese certainly won't have forgotten the goal he scored on 20 April 2011 in the final of the Copa del Rey at Mestalla in Valencia. It is the fans' favourite goal of the year – the one that brings Real their only trophy of the season. But it doesn't come for more than 100 minutes. Cristiano starts in the number 9 position, which is not where he feels most comfortable. At the end of an intense 90 minutes of excellent football, he has still only had one shot on target. He will have to wait until extra time to break his long-drawn-out dry spell against Barça. Di María plays a one-two with Marcelo and sets off on a run, beats Alves and unleashes a powerful cross from the left-hand side. Cristiano leaps into the air above Adriano and, demonstrating his ability to dominate in the box that he learnt at Man United, sends the ball flying into the net with a powerful header. Barça goalie Pinto can do nothing to stop the shot. The spectacular goal brings home Real's first Copa del Rey in almost two decades. What of Messi in this match? 'He was desperate. He tried to get things going from wherever he happened to be in the attack, but with no luck,' says newspaper *El País* in its evaluation of his performance. 'His zigzags invariably landed him in the clutches of the Real players. The Flea was controlling the play far too much – in the first half the team hardly passed the ball at all. After the break everything changed and the deep passes to Pedrito were excellent. Unfortunately, the solitary goal was ruled offside. In the end, he took advantage of his position as a leader, trying to control the play too much, and this allowed Real Madrid to make a comeback.' It is a fair assessment, and it is also the first defeat in a final for Barça under Guardiola.

And let's not forget the match at Nou Camp the following year, in which Cristiano breaks the 1–1 deadlock in the 73rd minute to seal the 2011–12 La Liga victory for Real.

When it comes to Leo, it's impossible not to mention his performance on 27 April 2011 at the Santiago Bernabéu in the first leg of the Champions League semi-finals, which takes Barcelona through to the final at Wembley and their fourth trophy. Two successful moves and two goals by the Argentine bringing down a Real Madrid team which has resorted to conservative tactics and possessive guarding of the area. Right from the start, the Whites try to stop Messi playing his game, but they don't make any attempt to play their own. So much so that after a quarter of an hour, Cristiano Ronaldo is signalling desperately to his teammates to move out of their positions so that he can play with them, and so that they can create chances for him. At the end of the first half, he is the one who creates the most dangerous opportunity for Real. He launches the ball from distance, creating plenty of difficulty for Valdés – difficulty matched only by a shot from Özil later in the game. But at this point, Ronaldo's attempt is their only chance worth mentioning. At the other end, Messi is playing as deep as midfield, being kept far away from the box where he can do the most damage. He keeps himself busy with runs which go nowhere. But things change in the 60th minute when

Pepe comes down with full force on Dani Alves's leg. He is immediately shown the red card. Barça now have eleven men against Real's ten, and Leo is able to get into the opponent's area. In the 77th minute, buzzing between white shirts like a careless wasp around the edge of the area, he takes a shot. It's deflected, Xavi retrieves it and passes it out to Afellay on the wing. The Dutch midfielder makes a run and crosses it in towards the penalty spot. Messi gets there first, beating Sergio Ramos to the ball. He taps it into the goal with his toe and it's 1–0. Ten minutes later the Flea performs his encore. This time it's magnificent: he leaves the centre circle, passes to Busquets who passes it back, sets off on a slalom leaving Ramos behind and, breaking free from Albiol, changes direction, gets into the box, dodges past Marcelo and, before Ramos can catch him, he finishes it off in spectacular style. Game, set and match. He is certainly the master of this particular match.

One more *Clásico* worth mentioning: the final of the 2011 Spanish Super Cup, where Leo scores four of the five goals that give the *Blaugrana* their first title of the season. Two in the first leg on 14 August at the Bernabéu, and two more in the return leg at the Nou Camp on 17 August.

The match on 16 April 2014 sees the most talked about moment between the two players of all the *Clásicos* to date, as the *Blaugrana* and the Whites come face to face in the final of the Copa del Rey at Mestalla, a match in which Real triumph 3–0. But the impressive result is hardly noteworthy compared to the image of the night: Cristiano consoling Messi. The Portuguese hasn't been on the pitch due to injury niggles, but that doesn't stop him going over to the Argentine in an attempt to cheer him up following a bitter defeat.

The next time they meet on the pitch is on 25 October 2014 at the Santiago Bernabéu. For the first time, the match unites Barça's new strikeforce of Leo, Brazil's Neymar and Uruguayan Luis Suárez, who debuts with his new team following an eight-match ban for biting Italy's Chiellini during the World Cup. But the triple aces are rendered powerless against the Real effect, and the Whites take the first duel of the season 3–1 thanks to a comeback led by Ronaldo.

The roles are reversed on 22 March 2015, the second *Clásico* of the season, as the rival teams head out onto the Nou Camp pitch at 9pm. This time it's the Whites who start off well, but in the eighteenth minute the *Blaugrana* take advantage of a dead ball to get ahead. Messi passes to Mathieu, who heads it in to make it 1–0. Cristiano gets the equaliser, but ten minutes after the half time break Suárez makes it a definitive 2–1. Leo doesn't score, but he does set a record for the most assists in the history of the *Clásico*.

It's much the same story eight months later, in the 2015–16 season. It's Saturday 21 November, and Barça are away to Real. Leo has been given the all clear by the medics after six weeks out due to injury, although he is still starting on the bench. He comes on in the second half ... and he doesn't disappoint. The Catalans crush their eternal rivals 0–4, their best *Clásico* victory since 2009.

With the memory of that triumph still fresh, Barça go out onto the Nou Camp pitch on 2 April, just a few days after the death of legendary *Blaugrana* player and coach Johan Cruyff. It's a blow for the whole team, who hope to be able to pay tribute to him with a resounding victory over Real in the second *Clásico* of the season. The game starts with a video honouring the late footballer, and a mosaic created by the fans in the stands, depicting his number 14 shirt and the words 'Graciès Johan'. Unfortunately, the result gives them no cause for celebration. The locals go one up in the 55th minute, but Real manage to get back on track thanks to a Karim Benzema equaliser in the 62nd minute. And a stunning shot from Cristiano takes it to 1–2: he gets the ball from Gareth Bale, controls it perfectly on his chest on the edge of the box, and shoots, sliding the ball under the legs of goalie Claudio Bravo. Real have succeeded in breaking a run of 39 games without loss for the *Blaugrana*.

And what about their clashes with their respective countries? Interestingly, they have only come face to face twice, both times in friendlies. The first is on 9 February 2011 in Geneva. The enormous sense of anticipation surrounding the match means the 33,000 tickets are sold out in minutes and are soon going for at least €600 online, six times the original price. The match will be broadcast across five continents and will be followed by 250 journalists from sixteen countries. Leo and Cristiano have decided not to make pre-match statements, while the two coaches try their best to emphasise that this match is Portugal versus Argentina, not Ronaldo versus Messi – with little success.

Referee Massimo Busacca blows the whistle and seven-time world Formula One champion Michael Schumacher takes the honorary first kick. After nineteen minutes of play, Messi delights the crowd with one of his famous slaloms. He takes off from the left-hand side of his own half, dodges past opponents, and offers the ball to Di María with a sharp pass which evades the Portuguese defender. The Real player fires the ball into Eduardo's goal: 1–0 to Argentina. Shortly afterwards Cristiano equalises, more by chance than through any great work of his own. On the edge of the area, Nani manages to confuse the Argentine defence. His pass doesn't quite reach Almeida and the ball ends up dead in front of goal. Cristiano only has to beat Romero to the punch to make it 1–1. Now the fans have really got themselves a show and it's clear who the real stars are. The other twenty men on the pitch are secondary by comparison. But in the 60th minute, Portugal coach Paulo Bento replaces Cristiano with Danny.

The Portuguese think the match is more or less over. But Argentina are hungry for results, and they push forward in search of the victory. In the final minute, Coentrão wins a penalty, giving Messi the chance to score, win the match, and level the score with Cristiano.

Three years later, it's time for the rematch, on 18 November 2014 in a friendly at Old Trafford. Ronaldo has just become the record goal-scorer in European Championship history with a total of 23, including qualifying matches and finals tournaments. On 14 November he overtook Denmark's Jon Dahl Tomasson's total with a goal that helped Portugal to a 1–0 victory over Armenia. The Portugal captain is also currently his country's top scorer of all time, with 52 goals in 117 matches. But both he and the Flea are lacklustre today, and Cristiano ends up coming off at half-time. The spectators forgive him, offering a huge ovation to the player who lit up their pitch for six years with Man United. And in case there is any doubt about their loyalties, they throw the odd 'boo' in Messi's direction too. In the end Portugal win 1–0 with a goal from Raphaël Guerreiro.

CR7 versus Messi has earned its place as a classic derby. For several years they have been at the forefront of a historic rivalry which has only spurred them to become better footballers and athletes. There is a joke that has circulated online that perfectly sums up the incessant comparison of this eternal duel. The two footballers are sitting on a sofa, chatting. 'God sent me down to Earth to teach people how to play football,' says Cristiano Ronaldo. 'Don't be daft, I didn't send anyone down to Earth,' replies Messi.

Chapter 6

Goals

Cristiano Ronaldo
Goals: 604 (with clubs and country) as of 28 June 2017

Lionel Messi
Goals: 581 (with clubs and country) as of 22 July 2017

* * *

They are perfect goal-scoring machines. Until they burst on to the European footballing scene, no one had ever scored as many as they have. In a single season these two stars can each score more goals individually than some entire teams in the Spanish top division. And every year they set new records. The Portuguese is the top goal-scorer in the world in terms of volume, whether counting just club goals or whether including international goals as well. He is the top scorer in European club football (108 goals). He is the highest goal-scorer in the history of the UEFA European Championships (29 goals for Portugal across all qualifiers and finals tournaments). And he is also Portugal's top scorer of all time (75 goals).

He is also the only player who has managed to score at least 50 in six seasons – consecutive seasons, no less (from 2010–11 to 2015–16 inclusive). He is the only person in the history of the Champions League to score at least ten goals in six consecutive seasons (2011–12 to 2016–17 inclusive). He shares the record with Alan Shearer for the most goals scored in a Premier League season (31 in 38 matches in 2007–08). He is the only footballer in Man United history to have won the European Golden Shoe and the FIFA Puskás prize for the best goal. He was the first to score 40 goals in one season of La Liga (2010–11). He is the only player to have scored in six consecutive Real Madrid–Barcelona *Clásicos*. He holds the record for the most hat-tricks in the Spanish league (32 in total), and the Real Madrid record for the most goals in a calendar year (69 in 2013). And he is the highest La Liga scorer in away games (119 in total) with Real Madrid.

Leo Messi holds the records for the most goals scored in competitive matches during a calendar year (91 for club and country in 2012) and in a season (82 in 2011–12). He is the top club goal-scorer in a calendar year (79 in 60 matches in 2012) and the top club scorer in a single season (73 in 2011–12). He holds the record for the most goals scored in a single Champions League match (five goals against Bayer Leverkusen on

7 March 2012, a record now shared with Luiz Adriano). He has overtaken Gerd Müller's record for being the top scorer in the Champions League the most times (five times, from 2008–09 to 2011–12 inclusive and 2014–15). Lionel is the top scorer with the Argentine national team (74 goals). He has scored the most goals as captain, and he is the youngest player to have scored in an Albiceleste shirt in a World Cup (Germany 2006). In La Liga, he is the top scorer in history (349 goals in 382 matches), the top scorer in a single season (50 in 2011–12) and the top scorer in the history of Barça–Real *Clásicos* (23 goals in 34 matches). He is the first player to score 500 goals for a single club in the entire history of Spanish football (counting competitive matches and friendlies). He has also scored the most goals in the history of the Spanish Super Cup (twelve in fifteen matches). And finally, he is the top scorer in the history of FC Barcelona counting competitive matches and friendlies, and the club's top scorer in international competitions.

And there's more, because Messi and Ronaldo also share four records: the highest number of goals scored in international matches in a year (25 for club and country), the most hat-tricks in the Champions League (seven), the most hat-tricks in a season of La Liga (eight), and they are the only two players who have ever scored against every other team in the Spanish championship in a single season. In addition, they take it in turns to hold the record for top scorer in the history of the Champions League (as of 24 July 2017, CR7 is in the lead with 105 goals to the Argentine's 94).

These are undoubtedly breathtaking statistics, particularly as they are neck and neck in so many aspects. Although CR7 has scored more goals to date, he began his top division career two years before the Flea (he is two years older). There is one particularly intriguing parallel: they both experienced a goal-scoring breakthrough in their fifth season of playing professional football.

For Leo and Cristiano, scoring goals is as natural as drawing breath. Of course, not all goals are created equal, and of all the goals they have scored over the years, some have carried more weight than others. There are goals that have decided a result, there are goals that are simply stunning, and there are those that are particularly symbolic. Here are six of the most memorable.

Leo Messi: Barcelona vs Getafe, Copa del Rey semi-final, 18 April 2007

'Twenty years, ten months and 26 days later, Messi repeats Maradona's goal,' reads the headline on the front page of Madrid sports paper *Marca*. The morning after the 2007 Copa del Rey semi-final, the press is bursting with headlines, commentaries and linguistic inventions of all shapes and sizes, from 'Messidona', to 'The Foot of God', and 'Messi shocks the world'.

Here's what they are all shouting about: in the 28th minute at the Nou Camp, Leo Messi runs 65 yards, dodges round four opponents and the goalie, shoots with his right foot – unusual for him – and scores. For everyone watching, it immediately evokes the 'goal of the century' that Diego Maradona scored against England in the quarter-finals of the 1986 Mexico World Cup.

The 53,599 Nou Camp spectators are on their feet, grabbing hold of anything that can be waved, from the newspaper to the programme, a handkerchief or a scarf, waving en masse. And those who do not have anything of the appropriate colour still partake of the collective ritual, applauding until their hands hurt. A full-blown tribute. On YouTube, the goal stirs up plenty of debate. It is viewed thousands of times, as well as alongside Maradona's goal. It opens up an online debate as to which of the goals is better. Everyone has their own opinion, from expert ones to impassioned ones, while the media compares the two clips from every possible perspective, praising Leo's performance. 'Was Messi trying to imitate Maradona? Was it or wasn't it a big coincidence?' The man of the hour plays it down. 'Perhaps the play was similar, I have only seen it once on television,' declares Messi, 'but I never thought it could be the same as Diego's goal. They told me afterwards, but at that moment I wasn't thinking about anything, only of the joy of having scored a goal.'

Cristiano Ronaldo: Porto vs Manchester United, Champions League quarter-final, 15 April 2009

The first leg at Old Trafford finished 2–2, so the return leg at the Dragão Stadium will be crucial. Current title holders United are going for broke from the first minute. And it only takes six minutes to net the deciding goal. It's Cristiano who puts them through to the semis, getting hold of the ball in the centre of the pitch and unleashing an incredible shot from 30 yards that curls into the corner. Goalkeeper Helton da Silva Arruda dives and stretches as far as he can, but it's out of his reach. Ronaldo's teammates rush over to pile on CR7 in celebration. He looks serious, avoiding any big celebratory gestures, but conscious that very few players are capable of pulling off a move like that. It's the first time an English team have beaten Porto on their home turf.

Sir Alex Ferguson describes Cristiano's goal as 'magnificent' and 'sensational'. The goal ends up winning the inaugural FIFA Puskás Award, established in honour of Ferenc Puskás, for 'most beautiful' goal of the year. It garners 17.68 per cent of the votes as fans deliberate online between a shortlist of ten goals chosen by a panel of experts. CR7 accepts the trophy from Erzsébet Puskás, the widow of the legendary Hungary and Real Madrid player who was one of the top scorers of the

20th century. 'I wasn't expecting to win anything today,' he says after the ceremony. Several years later, the same goal will be voted sixth best as part of a 60-year celebration of UEFA. Although if you were to ask Ronaldo himself which he considers the best of his career, it would be this next one ...

Cristiano Ronaldo: Barcelona vs Real Madrid, La Liga 2011–12, 21 April 2012

It's a goal worthy of a Liga trophy. It's 8.00pm at the Nou Camp. For the first time since La Liga 2008–09, the Whites have made it to the end of the season ahead of the *Blaugrana*. They are four points clear of Guardiola's team, 85 to 81, enough to seal the championship at the home of their rivals and end Barça's incredible three-season run. All the attention is on Ronaldo and Messi. 'The battle for La Liga isn't about two teams, it's about two players,' claims Barça sports paper *Sport*. And it's not hard to see why: Ronaldo and Messi's performances have carried their teams this year. In 32 Liga matches, they have each scored 41 goals, equalling Ronaldo's 2010–11 record. 'You've never seen anything like it. Never has La Liga had two such phenomenal players,' continues *Sport*. With the exception of the 2011 Copa del Rey final, Ronaldo has generally lost up until now when going head to head with Messi – be it at Man United or Real. But on this occasion it's a different story, as he proves decisive. He scores the winner in the

2–1 victory, putting Mourinho's team seven points clear of their rivals. It's enough to ensure the title win. The goal comes in the 73rd minute, shortly after the equaliser from Alexis Sánchez, breaking the flow of Barça's attempted comeback. Mesut Özil gets the ball from Di María in front of the halfway line and crosses deep towards Cristiano. He breaks away from Mascherano and approaches Víctor Valdés. He sends the ball to the right, beating the goalie at the near post. It's an incredible shot, and he celebrates by running towards the Barça fans, signalling for them to calm down, mimicking the gesture Raúl once made towards them. 'Calm down, calm down, I'm right here,' he shouts, only too aware of what the goal symbolises. At the press conference afterwards he says: 'It was an important goal, but the team's victory as a whole was more important.' He has scored once again at the Nou Camp, playing a crucial role in breaking Real's three-year drought. And as far as the Madrid press are concerned, he has finally dethroned Messi.

Leo Messi: Barcelona vs Bayern Munich, Champions League semi-final, 6 May 2015

'These incredible goals remind us, once again, that he is the best. When he's on the pitch, we're guaranteed a victory.' So says Andrés Iniesta and, naturally, he is talking about the Flea. The Argentine has just sealed the semi-final against Bayern Munich, the team currently managed by Pep Guardiola, with whom Leo experienced the greatest period of his career. But he hasn't just played a starring role, he has also scored one of his most stunning goals, voted the best in the 2014–15 tournament by *Marca*'s online readers.

His touch of genius comes in the second half. It's 0–0 until the 77th minute, when Dani Alves steals the ball on the right wing, and passes to Messi who shoots from outside the box. 1–0. But that's not the goal in question. Three minutes later, he gets hold of the ball and faces up to Jerome Boateng, dodging round him so masterfully that the defender loses his balance and falls to the ground. Messi continues his run, and with a superb right-footed touch, subtly chips the ball to lift it over goalie Manuel Neuer. A true masterpiece. His teammates pile on top of him, euphoric, as the Nou Camp explodes into celebration. The match ends 3–0, with the Flea setting up the third goal for Neymar.

'Of course it's easier when Messi's there. He can do anything. We are reminded every day that he's on another level,' declares Barça coach Luis Enrique, with whom Leo has had his ups and downs this season. Even the Real fans, or at least some of them, acknowledge the incredible goal. 'I take my hat off to Messi today!' tweets two-time world rally champion, Dakar Rally winner, and die-hard Real fan Carlos Sainz.

And for Messi himself, it's a beautiful moment on the way to winning his fourth Champions League title.

Cristiano Ronaldo: Portugal vs Wales, UEFA Euro 2016 semi-final, 6 July 2016

A whopping 76.2 centimetres … an unforgettable jump that lifts CR7 above the height of Wayne Hennessey's crossbar, defying the laws of gravity. He is, quite literally, flying. 'It was like watching a basketball player going up for a slam dunk,' writes the *Daily Mail*. The whole play is over in just a few seconds: Portugal take a short corner, Raphaël Guerreiro crosses and Cristiano nets their first goal as the entire stadium looks on, open-mouthed. It's the 50th minute of Portugal's semi-final against Wales in the Euro 2016 tournament taking place in France. The header slams the ball into the net at a speed of nearly 45 miles per hour, catapulting the shot into UEFA's top ten best goals of the tournament. Just three minutes later, Ronaldo sets up Nani to make it 2–0. It's decided: Portugal will progress into the hotly anticipated final against the host nation. But aside from the goal the match leaves another abiding image: CR7 consoling Real Madrid teammate Gareth Bale. The Portuguese recounts: 'I congratulated him on Wales's incredible run. They have been a revelation. The rest of what I said to him is between us,' says the number 7.

Lionel Messi: Barcelona vs Roma, Champions League group phase, 24 November 2015

Leo is back on the pitch at the Nou Camp following an injury that has kept him off the pitch for six weeks …

and he's back with a vengeance. He scores two of the locals' six (it's 6–1 at the final whistle) but it's the first in particular that has the crowd on their feet. In fact, UEFA nominates it as one of the ten best Champions League goals of the season, while the media describe it as a 'true masterpiece of a team effort'. Every single Barça player has a hand in the play: 27 touches in 75 seconds. A perfect sequence, topped off by Lionel with a short sharp chip over Roma goalie Wojciech Szczesny. '*Ave* Messi, those who shall suffer, salute you,' writes sports paper *Marca* following the majestic performance that puts FC Barcelona through to the last sixteen of the Champions League.

Chapter 7

5–4

It's well known that it has been CR7's dream since he was little. And it becomes a reality in 2008: his first Ballon d'Or trophy. With 446 points out of a possible 480, he is the only player out of the 30 nominees to feature on every single one of the 96 jurors' ballot papers. He has beaten Messi by a landslide, with the Barça star amassing a mere 281 points. The Argentine has had a great season, but Barça have not won any significant titles. The international press have hailed Cristiano as the best in his class. From Beijing to LA, from Johannesburg to Reykjavík, the journalists called upon to vote by *France Football* – the French sports magazine which has been awarding the Ballon d'Or since 1956 – are unanimous in their praise of his talents.

Despite not shining in Europe, despite the ongoing soap opera at that time surrounding his possible move to Real, rumours about his personal life and his arrogance and provocation on the pitch, he has been crowned the winner. All that matter are his ability to put on a stunning performance, his enormous talent, the goals that earned him the Premier League Golden Boot, and the Premier League and Champions League titles he has won with United.

At 23 years of age, Cristiano has become the fifth-youngest footballer to take home the trophy. He is also the fourth United player and the first Premier League player since Michael Owen's win in 2001. The Portuguese knows that 2008 has been his year, despite his mediocre performances for Portugal in Euro 2008 (when he was undoubtedly playing with significant ankle pain). He defends himself in Italian newspaper *La Gazzetta dello Sport* a few days before the prize-giving ceremony: 'I think I have done more to deserve it than anyone.'

On 7 December an excited Cristiano heads to Paris with his whole family to collect the award. He is wearing a dark suit and tie and a grey and white shirt, with his hair slicked back. 'As everyone knows, winning the Ballon d'Or is something I have dreamt about since I was a little kid, which is why this is a very emotional and wonderful moment for me. I would like to take this opportunity to dedicate this trophy to my family, who are here with me,' he explains, turning and gesturing towards his loved ones. 'I dedicate it to my mother, my father, my sisters Elma and Katia, my brother Hugo, my closest friends Rodrigo and Zé, my agent Jorge Mendes … this is hard, there are too many people to mention … but I'm really happy,' he finishes. There are many people to thank, and there are still a few surprises in store at the gala. First, a video of Karim Benzema, Samuel Eto'o, Kaká and Luís Figo, among others, paying tribute to him. Then, Sir Alex Ferguson's speech: 'Cristiano deserves it and the club is thrilled with this latest success. Manchester United has been waiting for this moment for 40 years,' he says, adding that Ronaldo is exceptional and has matured so fast, to a point that even he couldn't have imagined five years ago. 'He is only 23 and has his whole career ahead of him.'

But neither Ferguson nor his protégé have reckoned with Messi, who would rain on the Portuguese's parade for the next four years. Starting the following year, Messi will go on to set a new record of being the first to win four Ballon d'Or trophies – and four consecutive ones to boot. The first, in 2009, he wins by a mile, receiving 473 out of a possible 480 points, more than double the score of Ronaldo, the runner-up, who has 233 points. Ninety of the award's 96 voters vote for Leo as their number one player, and with 98.54 per cent of the maximum number of points possible, nobody in the 54-year history of this prestigious prize has won it as convincingly or as near-unanimously as the Argentine. All sides are united in agreement on Messi's records, performances, talent, class and professional career.

'I cannot lie, I had a feeling that it could happen

this year – but the results of the ballot surprised me,' he says in the Barcelona press room after hearing the news. He is the first Argentine to win it, and the first winner to have trained at Barça's La Masia youth academy. 'This prize is an honour; it is wonderful and very special, but I wasn't obsessed with winning it. I knew that if it was meant to happen it would, but either way I would keep on working in the same way as always,' he explains. He accepts the award on 6 December at a ceremony in Paris, and admits to the audience: 'I would love to win it again. It would be magnificent to win one more.'

He gets his wish just over a year later, although this time no one is expecting it. At the gala in Zurich on 10 January 2011, Leo Messi is not the favourite for the 2010 Ballon d'Or. He is joined on the shortlist by teammates Andrés Iniesta and Xavi Hernández, who were crowned world champions in Spain's 2010 World Cup victory in South Africa. Pep Guardiola tears open the envelope, but the card inside is facing towards the audience, inadvertently allowing everyone to see the name, and the surprise is audible. A moment of confusion ensues while the coach turns it over, before finally announcing: 'Lionel Messi'. Days later, when the journalists ask about the rumours which had Andrés Iniesta tipped as the winner, Guardiola replies: 'I think Leo is the best.'

Dazed and confused, the kid from Rosario gets up

from his seat, buttons the jacket of his Dolce & Gabbana suit, adjusts his tie, sticks out his tongue like Michael Jordan after a great basket, and goes up on stage. 'Good evening and thank you very much for your applause,' he says, gripping the lectern. 'The truth is … I wasn't expecting to win tonight. It was already wonderful to be here with my teammates, and to win it is even more exciting. This is a very special day for me and I want to share it with my teammates and thank them, because without them I would not be here. I would also like to share it with the people I love, who have always supported me and are always by my side. And I want to share it with the whole of Barcelona and Argentina,' he says.

This year, for the first time, the trophy which *France Football* created in 1956 has been merged with the FIFA World Player of the Year award, which the footballing organisation launched in 1991, meaning that this year Messi has been chosen by journalists from all over the world, as well as the managers and captains of 208 national teams. The Argentine has been awarded 853 points (22.65 per cent of the vote), Andrés Iniesta 677 (17.36 per cent) and Xavi Hernández 637 (16.48 per cent). At 23, he is the youngest player to receive his second Ballon d'Or. But the choice of winner provokes a lot of criticism. 'I prefer to focus on the criteria required to award the Ballon d'Or … the World Cup has always been extremely significant in these types of awards – except in the year after Spain's win,' says Real Madrid and Spain captain Íker Casillas. 'The least I can say is that we've been unlucky. All the Spaniards are feeling slightly incredulous. I would have liked Andrés or Xavi to win, but we'll keep fighting for them to win it one day.' And almost all Spanish media outlets (except in Catalonia) voice their anger, along with many in France and Italy. 'Messi? Nooo!' reads the headline in *Gazzetta dello Sport*, summing up the general feelings of the Italian press.

For the tabloids, who had already crowned Andrés Iniesta as the winner, the Flea's second consecutive win is 'unbelievable' and 'unfair' because it 'doesn't reflect in the slightest' who the best player of 2010 really was. Messi's 58 goals in the last season, which helped Barça win their second consecutive Liga title and the Super Cup against Sevilla, seem to count for very little; likewise his brilliant start to the new season (28 goals in 26 matches). All that matters is the World Cup and the Champions League.

Fortunately, any doubts have dissipated by the following year, and on 9 January 2012 there are no complaints when Messi is crowned Ballon d'Or winner yet again, following an excellent twelve months. With his third consecutive victory he has equalled the tallies of Michel Platini (1983, 1984, 1985), Johan Cruyff (1971, 1972, 1974) and Marco van Basten (1988, 1989, 1992). He has entered the hall of fame. No one has ever won this type of hat-trick at the age of 24. Ronaldo is second, and Xavi third.

On hearing his name the Flea hugs Xavi, seated beside him in the Zurich Congress House, and goes up on stage. He is wearing a black bow tie and waistcoat and a wine-coloured velvet jacket – his usual Dolce & Gabbana. He seems much more relaxed than the previous year, when the excitement was overwhelming. He has no need to improvise his speech this year, unlike last year when he wasn't expecting to win. He hasn't written any notes, but he has thought about what he wants to say. No need to lean on the lectern to control his shaky legs this time either. After thanking the voters, his Barça teammates and the Argentina squad, he reserves a special mention for the *Blaugrana* number 6. 'Very importantly, I want to share this Ballon d'Or with my friend Xavi,' he says. 'This is the fourth time we have attended this gala together. You deserve it too. It is a pleasure to be by your side, here and on the pitch.' Clutching his trophy, Leo comments after the ceremony: 'I never dreamed I would win even one Ballon d'Or, let alone three. I mean, it's incredible and an honour, although I would never have achieved any of it without my magnificent teammates. That's why I shared it with Xavi. I hope we'll be able to keep it going for years to come, although it's a challenge. The most important thing is to maintain the level we're at now.'

Ronaldo is not at the gala as Real Madrid are playing Malaga the following day in the Copa del Rey. CR7 has pushed Xavi into third place with 21.6 per cent to the Spaniard's 9.23 per cent. But he is no match for Messi, who has received 47.88 per cent of the votes. The Real number 7 is back in the top three after a year of absence – a testament to his 40 Liga goals, which won him the European Golden shoe and helped Real to defeat Barça in the final of the Copa del Rey. But there's no beating the Flea.

The Argentine's future lies ahead of him, as Platini says: 'Messi is a killer player, he is strong and he will achieve many things. He is young, we have to let him work out his career path before we can know where he will end up. I don't know if he will overtake me, but he has many years ahead of him in football and he will continue to win many things.' Reflecting on the future, Leo says: 'I'd be happy to give up the Ballon d'Or for the next two years if Argentina could be the best in the world. Winning the World Cup in 2014 would be amazing – that would mean we are world champions. That would be the greatest thing ever.'

But he's back the following year, making history as the only player to win it four times, despite admitting it has not been his best year. He has only won a single title with Barça in 2012, the Copa del Rey. But he has broken a record: on 29 October he received his second Golden Shoe as the 2011–12 top goal-scorer in the European leagues, with a total of 100 points. Cristiano was second with 92 and Arsenal's Robin van Persie was third with 60. And in December he overtook Gerd Müller as the top goal-scorer in a single calendar year. Up until this point, no one had managed to beat the German's tally of 85, set four decades ago. Yet more records to Leo's name, at just 25 years of age. And when he accepts his fourth Ballon d'Or in Zurich on 7 January 2013, he is conscious of what an extraordinary moment this is, as he overtakes Cruyff, Van Basten and Platini. He has won 41.6 per cent of the votes, beating Ronaldo's 23.68 per cent. His goal-scoring achievements have counted for more than Cristiano's Liga or Super Cup victories with Real, or Iniesta's UEFA Euro 2012 trophy with Spain.

As in previous years, Leo stands out in a black Dolce & Gabbana tuxedo jacket with white polka dots and matching bow tie – quite a talking point. (The Spanish press will later publish his photo alongside one of Diego Armando Maradona in Seville in the early 1990s, wearing a similarly polka-dotted suit.) 'Good evening. In truth … it's incredible to be able to take home this trophy again. To win it for a fourth time in a row is truly amazing,' he says. After he comes off stage, he admits he voted for Iniesta, Xavi and Kun Agüero. 'Of course I could have voted for CR7, he's an incredible player. But I prefer to vote for my teammates.' In any case, as Ronaldo says: 'We don't compete on an individual level, it's all about football.'

It's yet another disappointment for the Portuguese, although he insists it is not a matter of life or death. 'Life goes on after the Ballon d'Or,' he declares. But when he beats Leo to the 2013 trophy the following year, it is clear that the award means a lot more to Cristiano than he would like to admit. In fact, he has to pause during his speech at the presentation ceremony, overcome with emotion. He dedicates his second Ballon d'Or to his family, as well as to Nelson Mandela and legendary Portuguese player Eusébio, who have both just passed away. 'This is an incredible honour. Everyone who knows me knows how difficult it has been for me to win this trophy,' he adds. After five long years he has reclaimed the Ballon d'Or, crowning him the best in the world. When he first won it in 2008, he was just 24 and seemingly unrivalled. But Messi's unstoppable rise began to highlight his own limitations. Four seasons, and a long and difficult wait for Cristiano have finally ended.

Years of hard work, goals and a slew of records have helped him win back the trophy from his eternal rival in one of the closest races in the history of the award. He has 1,365 points (27.9 per cent of the votes) to Messi's 1,205 (24.7 per cent). He has made it to this point thanks to perseverance, faith, sheer determination, and incredible goal-scoring ability, despite his lack of team titles. 'Cristiano has had a great year and he deserves the prize,' says Leo after the presentation.

And he has won it despite the fact that Sepp Blatter was betting on Leo. During an interview at the Oxford Union Society a couple of months earlier, the then FIFA president had compared the two players. 'Leo is a good boy. Every father and mother would like to have that at home. He's very good, he's very fast. He plays well, as if he is dancing. The other one [Ronaldo] is like a commander on the field of play.' Blatter stands to attention, imitating a soldier, and the audience laughs. 'One spends more on his hairdresser than the other, but I can't say who is the best. The shortlist for the Ballon d'Or comes out next Tuesday, and then it will be decided,' he continues. 'I like both of them. But I prefer Messi.'

A rather uncalled-for remark that, nonetheless, didn't stop CR7 from becoming the first Portuguese to win the trophy for a second time, and just the third to have won it at all, after Eusébio in 1965 and Luís Figo in 2000. The following year it's a similar story, as Blatter bets on Bayern Munich goalie Manuel Neuer, who helped Germany win the 2014 World Cup, but the rest of the world prefers Cristiano. He wins 37.66 per cent of the votes, more than his two rivals put together. Messi wins just 15.76 per cent, and Neuer is third with 15.72 per cent.

Unlike the previous year, Cristiano gets through the presentation without any tears, although he still looks very emotional at the gala on 12 January 2015.

'I don't want to tread water, I want to win as many as Messi. He hasn't thwarted my dreams, rather he has inspired me.' Leo is his reference point, the mirror he holds up against his own achievements. Even Cristiano Junior admires his father's biggest rival. 'He watches your matches and he talks about you,' CR7 tells the Barça star when they meet before the ceremony – an encounter that leaves his four-and-a-half year old son speechless. He has equalled Cruyff, Van Basten and Platini's tallies, but now he is aiming for Messi's.

But rather than diminishing, twelve months later the gap between the two stars widens once again. On 11 January 2016, Lionel arrives in Zurich as the strong favourite to lift his fifth trophy after a two-year drought. Even the Portuguese is conscious of the fact that, this time, there is an undisputed winner … and it's not him. 'I'm not surprised to be here, but Leo has the edge because his team won all the titles,' acknowledges Cristiano at the pre-ceremony press conference. Ever since they saw each other at the last gala a year ago, there has been a better understanding between the two. They seem relaxed, friendly – none of the tension. They are sitting next to each other during the ceremony, and there is no surprise when the winner is announced, but there are no negative reactions either.

Leo wins the 2015 Ballon d'Or with 41 per cent of the votes to Cristiano's 27 and Neymar's 7. He goes up on stage to receive the trophy from the 2007 winner

Kaká, wearing a far more sober suit than on previous occasions. He has swapped his usual eye-catching Dolce & Gabbana for classic Armani – a more mature look, reflecting his progression on the pitch as well. 'The nerves and excitement make it difficult to speak in front of so many people,' he says, with the trophy in his hands. 'It's a very special moment for me to have been able to win this once again, after two years seeing Cristiano win it. It's incredible that this is the fifth, it's far more than I ever dreamed of as a child.' Then it's time for the thank yous: 'I want to thank everyone who voted for me, and my teammates, because as I always say, this wouldn't be possible without them. And I want to thank football in general for what it has enabled me to experience, for the good and the bad, because it has helped me to grow.'

2009, 2010, 2011, 2012 and 2015 … no one has achieved anything quite like it, and no one ever imagined that anyone would. When it comes to Leo, it seems there are no limits.

Meanwhile Cristiano is also challenging the notion of limits, closing the awards gap between the two in 2016 – this time with two individual titles. In December, at a private photo ceremony at the Bernabéu, he receives his fourth Ballon d'Or from *France Football*, followed by the Zurich gala on 9 January 2017 where he is hailed as FIFA's Player of the Year, now renamed as 'The Best' award. 'There has been a lot of negativity and a lot of campaigns against me – both within and outside the footballing world. They try to attack me from every angle, but ultimately "The Best" prize was intended for the best player, and that's me,' declares an elated Ronaldo as he accepts the trophy from Gianni Infantino. He had received 34.5 per cent of the votes, while Messi had 26.4 per cent and Antoine Griezmann had 7.5 per cent. 'It will be almost impossible to beat this year. This is the high point of my career and I'm very happy.' Unlike in previous years, Messi does not attend the ceremony.

Aside from the Ballon d'Or, there is one other fiercely contested trophy: the European Golden Shoe, which since 1968 has recognised the leading scorer in league matches from the top division of every European national league. Here the score is 4–4. Cristiano won it in 2008 with Manchester United (31 goals), and then with Real Madrid in 2011 (40), 2014 (31) and 2015 (48). Only Messi has won it as many times as him, although Cristiano has won it in two different national leagues. Leo won it in 2010 (34 goals), 2012 (50), 2013 (46) and 2017 (37), all with Barcelona. For the time being, it's just yet another CR7–Flea contest that remains wide open …

Chapter 8

Playing style

'I play to be the best,' is Cristiano Ronaldo's well-worn phrase, but Leo Messi must surely have a similar mantra. Ambition is one of the few things that these two star players have in common. They are seemingly opposite in many other character traits, and it shows on the pitch. They each have their own way of controlling the ball, positioning themselves on the field, and interacting with the rest of the team. They represent two very distinct ways of playing the beautiful game.

According to Eduardo Gonçalves de Andrade, aka Tostão, Leo's style is 'minimalist'. The Brazilian footballing legend explains: 'He makes very few movements or gestures, only those that are absolutely necessary to do something extraordinary.' In other words, he is only interested in getting round his opponents and scoring. Like Pelé in his day, he never pursues a pointless run. He beats his markers with the sole objective of getting in front of goal. He is utilitarian, he has no interest in showing off his abilities. 'He's an unsettling player, he can disrupt a game with a single movement,' explains former

Fox TV commentator Fernando 'Chiche' Niembro. 'There are good footballers who can't do that over the course of 90 minutes. But with a single dodge or a single shot Leo is capable of stirring up the fans and the critics.'

And what about Cristiano? 'Cristiano Ronaldo subscribes to Euclid's theory: the shortest distance between two points is a straight line,' muses award-winning Spanish writer Manuel Vicent in *El País*. 'Not only that, you have to blast down that line at warp speed until you reach the goal. Leo Messi prefers Einstein: the shortest distance between two points is always a curve, and the only way to arrive is if you zigzag unpredictably like a careering swine trying to dodge the axe. Ronaldo inspires passion – Messi, admiration.' And that's why they are considered the gods of the modern footballing world. In the pursuit of absolute perfection, CR7 seems to subscribe to a classicist ideology. He has honed and refined his style, eliminating any blemishes and retaining the brilliance until he has crafted the perfect way to win matches.

Both have demonstrated that they have equally valuable playing styles. Cristiano's style reflects the evolution of a player who moved from Sporting to Manchester United, and then to Real Madrid – three very different experiences and playing styles. Meanwhile, Messi's style reveals flashes of his Argentine heritage against the backdrop of the distinct, ingrained culture of having been raised at Barcelona.

They are both swimming in talent, but have very different qualities. Leo personifies agility, while Cristiano is all about strength, playing a much more physical game. That was evident early on, from his first days at Sporting. 'He was talented, he could play with both feet, he was incredibly fast and when he played it was as if the ball was an extension of his body,' says Aurélio Pereira, one of Ronaldo's first coaches at the Lisbon club. 'But what impressed me more was his determination. His strength of character shone through. He was courageous – mentally speaking he was indestructible. And he was fearless, unfazed by older players. He had the kind of leadership qualities that only the greatest players have. One of a kind. He had it all, and it was clear he would only get better.'

By contrast, Argentina's Pablo Zabaleta observes friend and teammate Messi's deft movements: 'As a player he's a gem. He has the heavenly gift of handling the ball really well. He impresses me with his ability to move the ball at such speed. It's incredible, what he's capable of doing, the way he gets round the other players, the way the ball is always glued to his foot. As he has shown us many times, he's capable of taking a team to greater heights, of deciding a match. And he doesn't feel the pressure.' Former Barça player Gianluca Zambrotta also recalls Messi's footwork: 'He has incredible ball control, it's always glued to his left foot, he's extremely fast, he moves well in small spaces with or without the ball, like Maradona. And he'll run rings around you to show you up. You never know where he'll go next. He could go to your right, to your left, or nutmeg you. He's in a class of footballers where, if he's on form, he'll win you the match.' Messi is one of the few players in the world who can drive the ball forward without looking at it, and that allows him to watch the opposition and his teammates, and make an unprecedented pass. He can do it because he sees the whole pitch. He has a lot of precision while at the highest possible speed. He plays imaginatively, he's creative and every time he gets the ball, every time he challenges the opposition, it's an experience … everyone is waiting for something to happen. And it does. Messi has physical thinking. He is mind and body, all at the same time. He has the same gift that Pelé, Maradona and Di Stéfano had. It's the speed with which his brain tells his legs what to do.

In addition to his agile movements, Messi is known for being extremely precise, even at top speed. So much so that Dutch researcher Pieter Medendorp, professor at the Radboud University in Nijmegen, has studied the player's brain to try to understand how he manages to make decisions in a fraction of a second. 'Messi makes the decision to run, jump or shoot in an instant, and we want to understand what is going on in his brain when that happens,' says Medendorp. 'What makes him opt for one route and not another? On the pitch,

A young Cristiano at Sporting
Lisbon in November 2002.
Antonio Cotrim/AFP/Getty images

Two years later, Ronaldo is
with Manchester United and
Lionel Messi is making his first
appearances for the Barcelona
first team.
Francesc Valcarcel/Press Association
Images

Messi scores against Ronaldo's United in the 2009 Champions League final.
It is the first time the two superstars have faced each other on the pitch.
Shaun Botterill/Getty Images

Cristiano shoots to score in the final *Clásico* of 2011–12, winning the match
and sealing Real's first Liga title in four years.
Denis Doyle/Getty Images

the Real staff are convinced that moving him into the centre won't be too traumatic. 'He is tall, strong, can head the ball, and plays well with both feet … he has everything he needs to be a great centre forward,' a Real Madrid source is quoted as saying in *Marca*. The coaches know Cristiano will have to be on board with the idea, but they believe it will enable him to play for many more years in the future, when his speed and strength diminish over time. 'Cristiano Ronaldo is one of the best players of all time, he is one of the best strikers in the history of football. I have never coached anyone better than him,' writes Ancelotti some time after departing the Real Madrid dugout. 'He will always find his place, because he has a special talent for moving around the pitch. He needs to be allowed to feel free at any moment and in any position. Cristiano's free style of attack is a positive thing because it's what makes him even more unpredictable.'

Barça have also got alternative plans for Messi, and curiously they involve doing exactly the opposite: pulling his position further back. He will still form the centre of the *Blaugrana* attack and will still have plenty of freedom of movement, but it is intended to allow him to use his physical force more sparingly. The club want to protect him from unnecessary exertion and reduce the 30- or 40-yard solo slaloms that he is known for but which will take their toll on his fitness over the course of many years. They believe a new formation will increase Leo's ability to read the match and contribute more to the efforts of the team as a whole.

It's one of the greatest challenges for both players: focusing more on the team and less on individual opportunities on the pitch. They have had to overcome something that is an Achilles heel for many great players. 'The same thing happens with Leo that used to happen with Maradona, he's an individual who carries such weight that he can manage without the team,' Argentine Jorge Valdano, former director general of Real Madrid, said during the star's early years at Barcelona. 'He's not like Zidane or Platini, who need the team around them in order to display their collective intelligence. Messi needs his teammates to pass him the ball, after that he does the rest on his own.' Although, interestingly, Maradona obviously didn't recall what a challenge it can be for a player to overcome the tendency towards individualism, claiming back in 2008 that Leo focused more on himself than on the Argentine team: 'Sometimes Messi plays for Messi. He still forgets about his teammates. If he played better with Sergio Agüero or Juan Román Riquelme, it would throw off his opponents more.' When Ronaldo arrived at Real he was accused of much the same thing. 'Cristiano Ronaldo has always been like this, arrogant and individualistic on the pitch, that's the player Real Madrid have signed,' claimed journalist Sara Carbonero, partner of former Real goalie Íker Casillas, now with Porto.

But the tide has shifted in recent years, and the two stars have gone from being brilliant soloists to being much more sensitive to the needs of their teams – although from time to time they can still be drawn in by their innate goal-scoring instincts. Ronaldo seems to get on better with his teammates, he gets more involved in defensive play and knows how to read the match better. In fact, he's the one who has been frustrated by other players' soloist tendencies, as happened when Gareth Bale joined Real. In more than one match, the Portuguese has been seen gesticulating indignantly because the Welshman hasn't passed him the ball when he was in front of goal. And in Messi's case, what more proof is needed that he is focused on team playing than his record of having the most assists in La Liga over the last 25 years. That particular record came in February 2015 in a match against Levante when he set up a goal for Neymar, overtaking Luís Figo, who had 105 assists. 'Leo is capable of being the Golden Shoe, the Pichichi and scoring ten goals a second, but he is extremely focused on playing as a team – he and all his team-mates,' says current *Blaugrana* coach Luis Enrique.

Interestingly, he seems to concur with one of the most controversial managers in Real Madrid's history: José Mourinho, who several years ago accused Leo of theatrics when he had to endure his talents from the dugout with the Whites or at Chelsea. Now he points to Messi when noting the importance of the group over individualism: 'On the one hand you have individualistic players. For example, Messi has won the Champions League under three different coaches. I think it's easier to win with him than against him. And although I know there are people who think that individualism is more important than the team, I persist in believing that the group is more important. But there is no escaping the reality: there are some players that make all the difference.'

Cristiano is also among those who make the most assists in the Spanish league. In the 2014–15 season, he created fourteen La Liga goals, the highest number of assists for a Real Madrid player. It's clear that both players have gained in emotional intelligence. They are more empathetic, proving that they continue to find new ways to be even better.

Chapter 9

The delivery boy versus the playboy

When it comes to personality, it seems they are chalk and cheese. Leo is shy and appears to want to blend into the background – very different from Cristiano. Leo is the boy next door, the 'delivery boy', to use the Argentine expression. The one no one notices, versus the one with a model physique who gets all the attention. The one who finds it hard to hard to fit in, versus the outgoing one who seems to have no problem making friends. At least, that's the prevailing image of the two stars. And while there is some truth to it, it is a lot more complex than that. In fact, Cristiano and Leo's personalities are a lot more similar than at first glance.

Of course, they share the same obsession with the ball. 'The worst punishment we could threaten him with was: "You're not going to practise today",' says Messi's mother, Celia María Cuccittini. '"No mummy, please, I'll be really good, don't worry, I promise … let me go and play," he begged and insisted until he convinced me. Leo wasn't a temperamental child and he wasn't lazy either, he's always been a good boy, quiet and shy, just as he is today.'

Neither of them enjoyed studying, or doing their homework when they got home from school. They always found a way to escape so that they could go and play ball with other kids in the street. 'When he got home from school, I used to tell him to go to his room and do his homework,' says Ronaldo's mother Dolores. 'He always told me he didn't have any. So I would go and start the cooking and he would try his luck. He would grab a yoghurt or some fruit, climb out the window, and run away with the ball under his arm. He'd be out playing until 9.30 at night.' And that's not to mention all the times he ditched school to play.

From a very young age their character traits were evident on the pitch. CR7 was just as competitive even then. If something didn't go his way, he made his feelings known. He cried and got angry very easily if a teammate didn't pass him the ball, if he or someone else missed a goal or a pass, or if the team wasn't playing how he wanted. That's exactly what happened in a match in the 1993–94 season when his team, Andorinha, was losing 2–0. 'Ronaldo was so distraught that he was sobbing like a child who's had his favourite toy confiscated,' says Rui Santos, the Madeiran club's president. 'In the second half he came on to the pitch and scored two goals, leading the team to a 3–2 victory. He definitely did not like to lose. He wanted to win every time and when they lost he cried.'

His mother Dolores explains: 'That's why he was nicknamed "cry-baby".' He was already so intensely ambitious that he didn't want to play against better teams because he didn't like losing. His father tried to reason with him by explaining that only the weak give up. It's clearly a lesson he has not forgotten.

Cristiano has always wanted to improve his game, in whatever sport he was playing, be it tennis, table tennis, pool, table football, darts, athletics, or a one-on-one test of speed. He has spent every waking hour working towards being the best. In the Real dressing room they have nicknamed him 'El Ansia' – the anxious one. 'His colleagues know that he dedicates himself body and soul to a long list of obsessions,' writes Spanish newspaper *El País*. 'His sit-ups, his eyebrows, his hair, his fight to ban cigarette smoke, as well as trophies, goals and, of course, the desire to win the Ballon d'Or.' He always wants more, and he doesn't hide it.

Messi also pushes himself, although it is not as obvious to outsiders. He has always been known for keeping himself out of the public eye, and everyone who knows him agrees that he is extremely reserved. He attributes it to genetics: 'My brother Matías is the same, and my father was also like that … My mother and Rodrigo are different.' Mónica Dómina, Leo's teacher from first to third grade, recalls: 'He was a quiet child, sweet and shy, one of the shyest students I have seen in my entire teaching career. If you didn't address him, he would sit silently at his desk, at the back of the classroom.' And some of his first teammates when he arrived at Barcelona remember how quiet he was, until around the time that the Barça B team won the Maestrelli Trophy in Italy in 2002. 'At first we thought he was mute,' says Chelsea midfielder Cesc Fàbregas. 'Then, thanks to PlayStation and that trip to Italy, we discovered that he knew how to talk.' 'Until that moment,' recalls Víctor Vázquez, another of the B team champions, 'he would always return to the dressing room, sit down in a corner, change, and leave without a word. But in Italy he began to gain confidence.'

There are times when his shyness makes the wrong impression, particularly during his early years with the Argentine national team. There is no shortage of anecdotes, like the time during training in Madrid when the coach invites the whole squad to a barbecue – an Argentine social ritual *par excellence* – in order to encourage group bonding. Leo does not open his mouth, not even to ask for some meat. It is a silence that is apparent and worrying to the others. 'They said that he didn't integrate into the group. They tore him to pieces. But it's not like that,' explains his childhood friend Cintia Arellano. 'Only someone who knows him knows what he feels. When he's not doing so well Leo is a little bit solitary, he withdraws, he retreats into himself.'

Even today, he lowers his eyes, smiling bashfully, when the journalists bombard him with questions or compliment his game. 'Only his intimate circle really know what he is like. It's not possible to know him just by meeting him or through official statements,' says Mariano Bereznicki, journalist at newspaper *La Capital de Rosario.* 'He seems to me to be incredibly humble. Fame and fortune have not changed him in the slightest. He is completely grounded.'

'When he debuted he was a very well-balanced person, calm, respectful and very shy,' says Frank Rijkaard, the coach who gave Leo his debut in the Barcelona first team. 'Over time, he has changed a lot, but without losing these attributes. Now he is more sure of himself. His attitude has not changed, but he is not the silent boy he was all those years ago. He is funnier, he likes to joke around when he is with his teammates or surrounded by people he knows.' And ex-Argentina coach Alfio 'El Coco' Basile affirms: 'He's a great lad. He's humble, he doesn't think highly of himself, he doesn't think of himself as a star and the fame hasn't gone to his head. He's a good person. He's the son every parent would like to have, or the one you'd want to date or marry your daughter. People everywhere love him and not just because he's an incredible footballer, but because of his personality.'

But not every aspect of his personality has been framed so positively. His relationship with his Barcelona teammates is constantly dissected and analysed in the press. And he has been referred to as the *triturador de delanteros* – best translated as the 'striker slayer' – because many who tried to play alongside him ended up leaving the club, having failed to build a rapport with him. The *Blaugrana* coaches always had their work cut out trying to build a strike force around him ... until the arrival of the Brazilian Neymar and the Uruguayan Luis Suárez. But the success of their alliance doesn't mean Leo's power in the dressing room has waned. In fact, as Suárez explains, he guides them: 'One day I moved into the number 9 position during a match and Messi told me to stay there,' recalls the ex-Liverpool player. 'Afterwards the coach saw we had found a good formation and he started to test it out.'

Though it may not be obvious at first glance, Leo is very much in control, and his gradual transformation since the early days now extends to his look as well – from a trendier haircut to the tattoos that now cover his entire right arm and half of his left leg, as well as his noticeably slimmer frame. He has bid farewell to pizza and barbecues and is now eating a lot more healthily. And he has been more prolific on social media. He is starting to project an image a lot more like Ronaldo's, with one small exception: the Portuguese does not have a single tattoo, which is rather unusual on a football pitch these days. In one interview, Cristiano claimed he didn't want any tattoos as it would prevent him being a blood donor. This is not strictly true, as it is possible to donate after waiting four months following a new tattoo, but it does highlight his more compassionate side. Because while CR7 loves his cars and his designer clothes, he is also big on humanitarian campaigns.

Meanwhile, the Portuguese is also known for being extremely meticulous and having an exceptional amount of willpower. He loves music, particularly reggaeton, as well as tennis, swimming, the number 7, and changing his hairstyle. And then there's table tennis, his favourite sport after football. He began to play as a child in Madeira, where the sport has a strong tradition and clubs compete on a national level. He kept it up while he was at Sporting and has played ever since. He loves going to matches, as well as playing against friends and teammates. He fancies himself as quite a good player, boasting on a number of occasions that the Sporting table tennis coach wanted him to join the team ... but he wanted to be a footballer.

In his obsessive quest for perfection, he is particularly conscious of what he eats. He doesn't eat junk food, and if he ever indulges he makes up for it with more exercise. In interviews, he is more open about himself than his Barça rival (though this is often perceived as arrogance), and if he ever gets angry, as he did in Las Vegas in the summer of 2015 when the press asked him an off-limits question about his rumoured departure from Real Madrid, he manages to make his feelings known without losing it completely. He is acutely conscious of his public image and of what is expected of him. As with Messi, the people closest to him are fiercely protective, ensuring that no unnecessary gossip is allowed to see the light of day. Family is everything to both these players. Their loved ones are everything to them, their pillars of support, their protective shields. They are the adored babies of the family.

And they are both young fathers themselves. Their sons were born 869 days apart, exactly the same as their fathers. Cristiano Ronaldo Junior is born on 17 June 2010, followed by Thiago Messi on 2 November 2012. But the similarities end there. Cristiano's mother's identity is unknown; it's practically a state secret. The only detail that is later uncovered is that she is Portuguese, not American as originally rumoured. It was Dolores who went to retrieve her newborn grandson from a Florida clinic while Cristiano was playing in the South Africa World Cup. The Aveiro clan's matriarch had learnt about the new arrival via an unexpected phone call. 'I'm having a baby and I want you to help me bring him up and take care of him, the way you have always done with me and my siblings. No one will ever know the identity of the mother,' Cristiano told her.

Leo becomes a father with his long-term girlfriend Antonella Roccuzzo. They are the same age and are both Argentine. They have known each other since they were five: she is the first cousin of Leo's childhood friend Lucas Scaglia. 'I have seen her grow up and she has seen me grow up. Our families know each other, so I didn't have any doubts,' the Barça number 10 has said. She studied dentistry and then communications before going to live in Barcelona with Leo. On 11 September 2015 their second child, Mateo, is born. They are a seemingly stable, extremely happy family. On 30 June 2017, Leo and Antonella get married at the City Center Hotel Casino in their hometown of Rosario, in a ceremony attended by 250 guests.

CR7's love life has been a bit more hectic. The press have always linked him to various different girls, and the list of his lovers and girlfriends, real or fabricated, is endless. A catalogue of English, Spanish, Brazilian, Colombian, Italian, Portuguese, Danish and Russian girls are said to have dated him. And the rumours continue even during the five years he is with model Irina Shayk – a relationship avidly followed through their social media channels, but which comes to an abrupt end in January 2015. It had been love at first sight when they met at an Armani photo shoot, although throughout their relationship they were always hounded by rumours of some rift or other.

At first the split seems civil, and the press claim it is due to the model's strained relationship with the footballer's family. But eventually Irina breaks the silence and hints that the separation may not have been as amicable as previously thought. 'I'm looking for a man who is honest and faithful,' she tells *E! News*. A few weeks later she is even more explicit in an exclusive interview with *¡Hola!* magazine in which she says she felt 'ugly and insecure' while with Cristiano. Once again she emphasises the importance of faithfulness and concludes that she thought she had 'found the ideal man ... but no.' Meanwhile the *Sun* alleges that the Portuguese cheated on Irina with at least twelve different women.

Ronaldo is rich, famous and good-looking, enjoys showing off his body and is not lacking in seduction skills. He is known as a ladies' man, a playboy who has allegedly seduced even Paris Hilton. Or at least, that's the image in the press. He insists that he prefers to keep his private life private, admitting: 'I have my romantic moments, I can be sensitive.' When it comes to women, he says he likes a nice smile, a good sense of humour, kindness and good conversation. 'Laughing is one of my favourite pastimes,' he has said. But let's not forget looks, which he says are 'important, very important, although the most important thing is what's on the inside, even when a woman is incredibly beautiful, like Angelina Jolie.'

In fact, it's a young Spaniard who looks remarkably similar to the *Tomb Raider* star who is next to capture the Portuguese player's heart – perhaps once and for all. Georgina Rodríguez is ten years his junior, but age doesn't seem to be an obstacle in their relationship. In contrast to Irina, who rarely attended official events with the player, Georgina has accompanied him on various occasions ever since the media first spotted them together in November 2016 on a holiday in Disneyland Paris. She is by his side when he is awarded FIFA's The Best award, she has been to several matches at the Bernabéu with Cristiano Junior, and she gets on well with family matriarch Dolores. At the Champions League final she can be seen celebrating on the pitch along with the other footballers' wives and girlfriends, and by mid-June the global press are speculating about whether she might be pregnant. Talking of babies, Cristiano has another surprise in store earlier in the month, when he takes to social media to announce the arrival of his twins, Eva and Mateo, born to a surrogate in the United States. 'So happy to be able to hold the two new loves of my life,' he posts, alongside a photo of him holding them in his arms.

Chapter 10

High points

'I have changed. It was a question of mindset. That came first, and everything else followed. It has changed the way I view a match. Before, if we lost or I played badly I wouldn't talk to anyone for three or four days while I got over the frustration. Now if we lose, I go home and see my son and I can let go. I might still be angry on the inside, but seeing him changes everything. Being a father has helped me grow up. It has helped me to stop being so obsessed over football and to realise that there are other things in life too.'

Leo Messi is quite emotional when talking about Thiago. All his triumphs, trophies and records pale in comparison when the little one arrives on Friday 2 November 2012 at 5.14pm at the USP Dexeus hospital near the Nou Camp. The Flea's younger sister María Sol is tasked with informing the world of the new arrival. Half an hour after the birth, she tweets 'Welcome little Thiago!!' Messi is a father. He had accompanied Antonella to the maternity ward at 9.00am, to a suite on the seventh floor where the whole family could have the maximum possible privacy. Jorge, Celia, Matías, Rodrigo and María Sol had arrived around 3.00pm. Leo is by Antonella's side and assists with the delivery. Everything goes well and both mother and baby are healthy. At 6.20pm, Leo posts on Facebook: 'Today I am the happiest man in the world, my son was born and thanks to God for this gift! Thanks to my family for the support! A hug to everyone.'

Thiago's arrival prompts other changes too. Messi seems much more open and relaxed about sharing his feelings. In fact, the day after the birth he goes out on to the pitch determined to share it with the world by dedicating his next goal to his son. He had already mentioned it a few hours earlier: 'I will do something special when I score the first goal, but then it'll be back to normal.' But as much as he tries, he doesn't score against Celta Vigo, and he has to wait until 7 November in a match against Glasgow's Celtic. He scores in injury time and sticks his thumb in his mouth in tribute. When asked why he chose such a low-key celebration in the end, he explains: 'The goal didn't really do much [Barcelona ended up losing 2–1]. There will be other chances to dedicate goals to him.' Plenty of other chances. On Sunday 11 November against Mallorca in La Liga, he is able to celebrate two goals and a victory – and the birth – in the way that he wanted. And on Sunday 25 November against Levante, he wears a wristband that reads 'I love you Thiago', which he kisses after scoring each of his two goals. 'Thiago is the most important thing in my life. I will always put him first. He is the best gift anyone could wish for, without a doubt.' And when the time comes to announce that the second baby is on the way, Messi is charged with letting the world know on social media. He posts a sweet picture of Thiago kissing his mother's growing belly with the message: 'We can't wait to meet you! Thiagui, mum and dad love you!'

On Friday 11 September 2015 Lionel misses training to attend the birth of his second son. Antonella posts the first photo of Mateo on Instagram, a black and white snapshot of baby and mother's hands, with the caption: 'Welcome my little boy! We are so happy to have you here with us! We love you! Daddy, Thiagui and Mummy #familyof4.'

Meanwhile, Cristiano Junior has an important role to play in one of the high points in his father's life. On 13 January 2014 in Zurich, Pelé opens the envelope containing the name of the 2013 Ballon d'Or winner. The cameras zoom in on the three finalists: Cristiano, Messi and Franck Ribéry. All three are focused on the stage. Pelé keeps them in suspense, smiling and waving the card, before finally announcing: 'The winner is Cristiano Ronaldo.' CR7 bows his head for a moment, then turns to kiss Irina, before making his way towards the stage. He shakes hands with then FIFA president Sepp Blatter, hugs Pelé, and greets Platini and the president of *L'Equipe* newspaper. And then there is a spontaneous moment which shows him at his most vulnerable – his son breaks away from his grandmother's arms and comes running up on stage to hug his father. Pelé picks the little guy up while Ronaldo accepts the Ballon d'Or trophy from Blatter. 'Good evening. There are no words to describe this moment …' he pauses, overcome with emotion. Tears in his eyes, a lump in his throat, he is unable to speak. The audience breaks into applause, giving him a moment to gather his composure and dry his eyes. He continues with a long list of thank yous, before saving the best for last: 'My girlfriend is here tonight, along with my mother and my son. This is the first time my son has seen his father win a Ballon d'Or … and … forgive me, this is a very emotional moment for me. It's difficult for me to speak. Thank you everyone.' The tears prove too much, and the ceremony ends with music and more applause.

As with Messi, Cristiano's son is his number one priority. He posts innumerable pictures of himself with Cristiano Junior on social media: on holiday, playing football, or simply spending a quiet day with the family. And Junior goes along to plenty of events. He is the most important thing in the player's life, far more than football. It's quite striking to see such a steely, determined athlete, used to handling himself in public, break down at such a show of affection from his son. 'They were real, genuine tears,' he will say later. 'When my son came up on stage my emotions got the better of me – even more so when I saw my family crying. I didn't want to cry, but I'm not made of stone.'

Just five months later, on 24 May 2014, CR7 experiences another unforgettable day as he lifts Real Madrid's tenth Champions League trophy at Lisbon's Estádio da Luz, a particularly special stadium for the Portuguese player. It's a magical moment, a just reward for an incredible season, in which Ronaldo has led his team on an incredible journey to triumph and to the trophy they have been dreaming of for twelve years. He doesn't give his best performance in the final against Atlético Madrid due to injury niggles in his left knee. But nothing – not even pain – is going to prevent him from scoring the final goal of the match. A penalty that gives him an opportunity to shine in every sense. Poor Thibaut Courtois, Atlético number 1. Goalie goes left, ball goes right. It was a goal which made no real difference as it came in the 120th minute when the score was already 3–1 to Real. Regardless, Cristiano celebrates as if it is the most crucial goal of his career, posing for the TV cameras, photographers, viewers and fans all over the world. Shirt off, hands on hips, a roar like the Incredible Hulk from Marvel's comic strip, his ripped biceps, pectoral muscles and abs tensed to the max. A little excessive considering that the other team had already been crushed and defeated. The reason for all this showing off? The iconic image was pre-planned. He needed it for *Ronaldo*, a documentary by Universal.

Why not make the most of such an opportunity to mix business with fun?

Ronaldo lifts the trophy six years after winning it with Man United. And he does it in the city where it all began, in the stadium where ten years earlier he cried in anger and disappointment after Portugal lost the Euro 2004 final against Greece. It's a golden moment for the ambitious striker, who has scored seventeen goals in the 2013–14 season, a Champions League record, despite having only played in eleven of the thirteen matches.

Having said that, Leo's Champions League performance the following year in the 2014–15 season will crown him the competition's highest overall scorer with 77, one more than the Portuguese. But if the Argentine had to choose a favourite moment in the season – and arguably his whole career – it would surely be Saturday 6 June 2015. It's 8.45pm at the Olympiastadion in Berlin, where Barça are taking on Juventus in the Champions League final. It's not the Flea's night to score, but he is undoubtedly a driving force and has a hand in all three goals. He is controlling all the play, despite the fact that every time he touches the ball, a crowd of Juve players surges towards him to block him. The first goal, by Ivan Rakitić in the fourth minute, is the third-fastest in a Champions League final. But the Italians get their own back after the break, equalising in the 55th minute. In the ten minutes that follow they are in complete control, piling on the pressure as the match becomes more and more intense. In the 65th minute Paul Pogba goes down in the Barça box, and for a few seconds Juve are more focused on calling for a penalty against Dani Alves than on the ball ... but it's denied and play rolls on. Then Messi gets the ball halfway up the pitch and goes on one of his runs, ending in a shot across the goalmouth. Buffon only manages to deflect it, leaving it open for Suárez. The Uruguayan comes charging in from the right and only needs one tap to net the second goal. And in the dying seconds of the match, Leo creates yet another opportunity, setting up Neymar to seal a definitive 1–3 victory.

Messi and Barça have made history. They have won La Liga, the Copa del Rey and the Champions League – their second treble in five years, something no other team has accomplished. And the formidable Messi-Suárez-Neymar 'MSN' strike force has netted 122 goals over the season. On the pitch, the Flea is seen burying the hatchet with *Blaugrana* coach Luis Enrique with a brief hug, perfectly summing up Barcelona's evolution this season, from a complicated start with public disharmony between the coach and the star player, to the grand finale that no one would have predicted even three months earlier.

Leo has recovered from all the criticism and interrogation and has reclaimed his untouchable position. 'Messi has been spectacular, he is our star player,' enthuses Enrique at the post-match press conference. It is the Rosarino's fourth European title, something very few players have achieved. The following day he posts a photo online of him having breakfast with the trophy. And during the celebrations with the fans back at the Nou Camp, he yells: 'We'll keep it up – we're hungry and we want to keep winning!' He is smiling broadly, enjoying this special moment.

Leo has cause to celebrate again just twelve months later. There has been no triple finale this season, but Barça still win two major titles: La Liga and the Copa del Rey. His joy at these latest triumphs is evident on his Facebook wall. 'Champions of La Liga!!! We did it thanks to a huge effort from everyone. We dedicate this title to our fans, who stuck with us until the end,' he writes on his personal account, alongside two photos, one of him giving the victory sign, and the other of the whole team. There has only been one glitch in the Argentine's excellent performance – getting knocked out of the Champions League too early.

Not so for his Real rival, who lifts the Champions League trophy for the third time in his professional career. But a far more important experience is yet to come for CR7, just a month later, undoubtedly the best moment of his career: UEFA Euro 2016 in France. The Portuguese's aforementioned spectacular goal against Wales in the semi-final clears the way for the ultimate test: a duel with the hosts on 10 July 2016.

The two teams head out onto the pitch at the Stade de France in Saint-Denis. The first few minutes pass with neither pain nor glory, but after barely a quarter of an hour the Madeiran gets a rough tackle from behind by Dimitri Payet. The referee doesn't see it and play continues. But not for Cristiano. It quickly becomes apparent that the number 7 is not OK. He is limping, and holding the affected leg. With each run it becomes clear that he is injured, until finally he falls to the ground. The medics bandage his knee on the touchline and he comes back onto the pitch. His teammates and his entire country can breathe a sigh of relief: it seems to have been just a scare. Ronaldo carries Portugal's hopes of making up for the final they lost against Greece in 2004. With him there, anything seems possible. Which is why, when the Portugal star is on the ground again just a few minutes later, asking to be substituted and unable to contain his tears, it seems as though that's it for Portugal. He comes off in the 24th minute, removing his captain's armband and crying inconsolably. Welshman Gareth Bale, CR7's teammate at Real Madrid, takes to Twitter to voice what many are thinking: 'Terrible to see Cris come off like that. Hope it's nothing too bad.'

Without the number 7, 90 minutes pass without any goals. It's the same story in the first half of extra time, before Éderzito António Macedo Lopes, aka Éder, becomes the hero of the match, making it 1–0 in the 108th minute and unleashing a collective euphoria. A bandaged Ronaldo, still limping, is on his feet following the last few moments of the match from the touchline, shouting instructions to his teammates. When the final whistle goes, the Madeiran goes back onto the pitch for the third time, but this time it's to celebrate. And shed more tears. He has finally achieved his greatest dream: winning a title with his national team.

It falls to him as captain to lift the cup, crowning Portugal as the best team in Europe. 'I always wanted to win something with Portugal, to go down in history, and now I've done it. I'm very happy, this is something I have wanted for a long time, since 2004,' he enthuses. 'This is what the Portuguese deserve, what the country deserves. I have always believed that these players had the courage, the ability and the strategy from our coach to beat France, and we did it. This is an unforgettable moment,' enthuses the star, conscious that this is something very few players achieve.

His latest momentous achievement, another one he will never forget, comes just one year later, this time with Real Madrid. Winning La Liga and the Champions League in the same season is something the club hasn't done since 1958, and what's more, Zidane's men are the first in the history of the Champions League to win two years in a row. 'It has been a unique season – winning La Liga and the Champions League, and we have an incredible team. It's been a phenomenal team performance, and on an individual level too. I worked hard so I could do well in the final stages and I scored some important goals. I'm very happy,' declares CR7 as he accepts the award for Champions League MVP, another one for his trophy cabinet.

Chapter 11

Low points

They are the best, the most admired, the most followed, the most desired. From the outside it seems like a charmed existence, where everything is perfect. But they have their ups and downs, just like everyone else. Here are some of the most challenging moments in Leo and Cristiano's careers ...

Starting with the Brazil 2014 World Cup final. Never in his worst nightmares has Messi imagined a final like this one. For nearly 120 minutes he is within reach of realising his dream of becoming a world champion with Argentina. But just when the whole world is convinced the match is heading into a penalty shootout, a surprise goal from Mario Götze brings Leo back down to earth with a bump. Germany have done it yet again. The *Mannschaft* are longstanding rivals of the Argentines, and they certainly know how to crush their dreams. They did it in humiliating fashion in the quarter-finals in South Africa in 2010, and they did it with penalties on German soil in 2006. The last time the two teams faced each other in the final was in Italy in 1990, and the Germans waited until the last possible moment to clinch the trophy on that occasion too, with a controversial penalty converted by Andreas Brehme in the 86th minute. It was revenge as much as anything. Four years earlier in Mexico it had been Argentina who had claimed their second World Cup – against who else but Germany. That was Diego Armando Maradona's World Cup, just as 2014 had been touted as Lionel Messi's World Cup.

The Barça player has been carrying the hopes and dreams of an anxious country on his shoulders, in the hope of repeating their 1978 and 1986 successes. He had one mission: to lead the national team to triumph just as Maradona did in his day. They are the two best players in the history of Argentine football. Even Maradona himself has named Leo as his successor. But they are separated by almost 30 years, and an enormous imbalance in terms of luck. Brazil has not gone as Leo hoped. For someone who always wins, coming second is a bitter failure.

In the match on 13 June 2014, Messi plays an uneven game, his performance reminiscent of his past season with Barcelona – a few flashes of brilliance, but no real magic. After such a promising start to the tournament, he is to leave Brazil empty-handed. He still wins the Golden Ball for player of the tournament, but it's as good as meaningless. And there is plenty of controversial debate about whether the Argentine even deserves the award. Some, including Maradona himself, feel that the thirteen wise men of FIFA entrusted with making the decision have opted for publicity over quality.

Unaware of the criticism – or perhaps sensing the controversy that surrounds him – Messi doesn't even make the slightest effort to smile when he goes up to collect the award. It has been mere minutes since referee Nicola Rizzoli blew the final whistle. Head bowed, Messi is trying to make sense of what has just happened at the Maracaná Stadium in Rio de Janeiro. He is barely even able to look Golden Glove winner Manuel Neuer in the eye when they shake hands before posing for the obligatory photographs. It makes for an interesting visual: eyes glued to the ground, Leo seems smaller than ever next to the Germany goalie. He also looks distinctly uncomfortable, not to mention lost in his thoughts, presumably going over every move of the match in his mind. He doesn't bother to hide his disappointment from the media. 'I don't care about the Golden Ball, I wanted to lift the World Cup.'

A year later it's a similar story when he is awarded best player of the Copa América, but this time he doesn't even go up to collect his prize. It's 4 July 2015 and once again the Albiceleste have come so close to victory, losing their second final in a row, and he doesn't want to fall into the trap of stirring up controversy again by accepting an individual award. He even looks uncomfortable going up to get his runner-up medal with the team, taking it off just after it is placed around his neck. This time, Argentina have been defeated by Chile, the host nation.

As in Rio the previous year, Messi has barely made an impact on the pitch in the Chilean capital, with the match ending up going to penalties. He has been fiercely marked throughout the match, and some of the local fans have even insulted his family from the stands. When it comes to the penalty shootout he scores his goal, while teammates Higuaín and Banega miss. Nonetheless, the Argentine people lay all the blame on Leo. He has been lacklustre throughout the competition, and he is lynched in the press and on social media. Sports paper *Olé* even demands that he relinquish the captain's armband. And, naturally, Maradona has something to say: 'We have the best player in the world, who goes and scores four goals against Real Sociedad, and then he comes here and barely touches the ball. Tell me, dammit, are you Argentine or Swedish?' The ex-Argentina coach adds that he's had enough of everyone going on about Messi needing to be coddled. 'Messi should be treated like any other player who puts on the national shirt. He's the best in the world, for better or worse. But listen, he didn't kill anyone, he didn't rape anyone, let's not turn this into a soap opera.'

What no one could have imagined – least of all the Rosarino – is that barely twelve months later fate would be against him once again. Leo has never hidden the fact that his biggest dream is to win a title with the Albiceleste: 'I would swap five Ballon d'Ors for a World Cup. Obviously. Team titles are always more important, and winning a World Cup is the highest achievement for any player,' he has said. And he has another chance to fulfil his dream of a title in 2016, during the Centennial Copa América in the United States. It's not a World Cup, but it's an important enough tournament that it would make up for it.

During the first stage, Lionel leads a solid team that have no problem making mincemeat of their opponents: 2–1 against Chile, a resounding 5–0 against Panama (with a hat-trick from the Albiceleste number 10) and 3–0 against Bolivia. Messi misses the opening match, and doesn't play a full 90 minutes, but his presence is felt from start to finish. In the quarter-finals they crush Venezuela (4–1) and then gave the hosts similar treatment in the semis, beating the United States 4–0. By chance, the line-up for the final on 27 June is exactly the same as the previous year: Argentina vs Chile. Everything points towards a different outcome this time round … until luck comes into play. During the match, the Barça striker gives it his all, but his team-mates squander three clear chances. When the final whistle goes it's 0–0, and there are still no goals after extra time. Once against, Argentina and Chile will battle it out on penalties. And once again, the Albiceleste will be going home empty-handed. This time Leo misses from the penalty spot, breaking down in tears immediately after his shot. A few minutes later, in the press area, he announces his departure without hesitation: 'This is a difficult moment, it's hard to analyse it. In the dressing room I felt that that was it, it was over for me with the national team. That's how I feel right now. It's a great sadness that it keeps happening. I missed an incredibly crucial penalty. That's it, it's better for everyone this way. We can't be satisfied with getting to the final and not winning. I have fought on many occasions and tried many times to be a champion with Argentina. It didn't happen. I couldn't do it.' After losing four finals (2007, 2015 and 2016 Copa América, and 2014 World Cup), Lionel is throwing in the towel and retiring from the Albiceleste.

'We were all screwed up. And the one who's the most screwed up is Leo. That's the worst I've ever seen him in the dressing room,' says Manchester City striker Kun Agüero. Immediately, the hashtag #NotevayasLeo – 'Don't go Leo' – goes viral. In his home country, no one has lost hope that the top scorer in the history of the Albiceleste will change his mind and come back to guide his team. And on 12 August 2016 that hope is realised when Messi confirms at a press conference that he is thinking of continuing with international football, backtracking on the idea of leaving the Albiceleste. 'I love my country and my national shirt too much. I see that there are problems with Argentine football and I don't want to create another one. I am grateful to everyone who wants me to continue playing with Argentina, and I hope that we can bring you some joy soon,' concludes the Flea.

Leo's life probably does deserve its own dramatisation – he's had his triumphs and his challenges. Perhaps the biggest challenge was his arrival in Spain all those years ago. He lands in Barcelona with his father on 17 September 2000. He is already well known on the Rosario football scene, where the papers dedicate double-page spreads to his achievements. Now, he has come to the Catalan capital to show that everything that has been said about him across the pond is true. And of course, he blows everyone away at his trial. 'I was coming straight from a meal and I arrived at the ground five minutes late. The two teams were already playing,' recounts Carles Rexach, who was Barça's technical director at the time. 'I had to run halfway round the pitch to get to the bench where the coaches were. It took me seven or eight minutes to get all the way round. By the time I sat down on the bench I had already made my decision. I said to Rifé and Migueli [the youth team coaches]: "We have to sign him. Now." What had I seen? A kid who was very small, but different, with incredible self-confidence, agile, fast, technically polished, who could run flat out with the ball, and who was capable of swerving round whoever stood in his way. It wasn't difficult to spot it; his talents, which are now known to everyone, were more noticeable at thirteen. There are footballers who need a team in order to shine – not him. To those who tell me that I was the one who discovered Messi, I always reply: if a Martian had seen him play they would have realised that he was very special.'

The boss is on board, it should be a done deal, but now comes the complicated part. First they have to sort out the actual signing of the contract. And not everyone at the club is so convinced. Some think Leo is too small and scrawny and think that all the fuss is just about a nifty little player. Plus, he's very young, perhaps too young, and they would have to find gainful employment for his parents. And the problems don't disappear once the contract is signed. The first few months of his new life on Catalan soil don't go particularly well. On 6 March 2001 Leo gets his provisional player's licence, but he is a foreigner and cannot play in any national competitions, which means he cannot join the children's A team, which should be his team: instead he has to make do with the children's B team, which plays in the Catalan regional league. To make matters worse, by March the teams are already formed and competing, and although he is good, it would be difficult – and unfair – to sacrifice one of the kids who has been playing since the beginning of the season in order to give him a place.

Another thing: his old Argentine club Newell's is not willing to make the necessary transfer arrangements so that Barcelona can enrol him in the Real Federación Española de Fútbol (Spanish Football Federation). And there is worse still to come. On 21 April a Tortosa defender tackles Messi hard: the result is a fractured left leg. It is the first injury in Leo's career. First he needs a splint, then a plaster cast and finally rehab – he won't be able to play again until 6 June. A week later it happens again. Another injury, this time while walking down the stairs – torn left ankle ligaments. Luckily this injury is less serious – he is out for three weeks.

His Barcelona experience has started off on decidedly the wrong foot. So much so that by the end of the season, for one reason and another, apart from practice matches Leo has only played in two competitive fixtures and one friendly tournament. Add to that all the other challenges that Leo and his family have had to face and things couldn't really get much worse for him. His little sister María Sol has struggled to adapt to their new life, causing his family to make the difficult decision to live apart just five months after their arrival. Leo's mother Celia returns to Argentina with María Sol, while Jorge stays in Barcelona with his sons. It's tough for Leo, given that he is already finding it hard to bond with his teammates due to his shyness. 'I knew that he was far from home, from his family, that he lived here with his father,' recalls Álex García, one of his first Barça coaches.

The family's separation prompts one of the most

difficult period's in Lionel's life, but having his father
with him makes things easier. 'We spend a lot of time
together, we're friends, although we have our ups and
downs,' says Leo. For Jorge it has meant transition from
skilled labourer to manager, under the name of Leo
Messi Management: 'It has not been easy, I have had
to learn the ropes. I have figured it out along the way.
I have had to shield him for his own good from the
expectations of people who might do him harm.'

Ironically, he has not been able to shield his son
from himself. Jorge is in charge of managing the player's finances, and the Spanish tax authorities believe
that not everything is in order. In 2013, the public
prosecutor charges him and Leo with failure to declare
earnings made through image rights between 2007
and 2009. According to the charges, the Messis owed
4.1 million euros in unpaid tax, a sum which has now
been paid up, with interest, to the courts, in the hope
of mitigating any punishment. But the payment does
not help them avoid a court appearance, which takes
place on 2 June 2016, just a few days before the start of
the Centennial Copa América.

Leo reiterates his position to the judge: 'My father
deals with the money, I play the football.' In his fifteen
minute statement he insists that 'I trusted my father
and the lawyers we had hired to take care of things.
At no point did it occur to me that they would dupe
me.' Lionel acknowledges that he would go along to

a notary's office to 'sign things', without really know-ing the details. He kept his enquiries to the bare mini-mum and his father filled him in only briefly. 'I knew we were signing agreements with sponsors who were giving X amount of money. And that I had to do publi-city appearances, photos, that sort of thing. But I have no idea where the money was going.' Jorge confirms this, asserting that the player was not aware of anything. 'We gave him the documents and he signed them.' But the family patriarch is also pleading his own case, insisting that he completely trusted his accountants. According to him, they were the ones who created a corporate structure based in tax havens without Jorge's knowledge, in order to avoid tax on Leo's image rights earnings. But the state attorney is having none of it. He is convinced that the Flea knows more than he was willing to admit, and he makes a scathing accusation: 'I don't want to compare Messi with a "mafioso", but it is as if he was the "capo" of a criminal structure,' he ventures. The verdict is handed down on 7 July 2016: father and son receive 21 months in prison for fraud, a sentence that their lawyers are appealing.

And while that case has been going on, there is another issue pending which could end up in the courts … the player's name is one of the first to surface in relation to the so called 'Panama Papers'. According to the leaked information, he and his father formed a shell company in Panama that allegedly served as a tax haven for his image rights deals. The family quickly releases a statement denying any wrongdoing. 'The Panamanian company referred to in the reports is a completely inactive company, which never held open accounts nor funds and which comes from the former company structure put in place by Messi's previous financial advisors, the fiscal consequences of which have already been normalised, with all the income that comes from exploitation of his image rights, prior to and after the procedure carried out in the courts, having been declared before the Spanish Treasury.' For now, the Treasury is investigating the accusations unearthed by the Panama Papers. Their veracity is still unconfirmed. Nonetheless, the player's image has once again been caught up in uncertain financial matters.

* * *

Cristiano Ronaldo had a particularly difficult first few years of his career, just like Messi. The Portuguese faced similar challenges, leaving Madeira and moving away from his family at just twelve years of age to pursue his dream at Sporting Lisbon. 'It was very hard. It was the most difficult time in my sporting career,' he will say years later. 'My sisters and my mother were crying. I was crying. Even when I was on the plane and we had just taken off, I thought of my family crying about me and I started to cry again.'

The first day of school is a traumatic experience. Ronaldo is late to class and the teacher is already taking the register. As he stands up and recites his name he can hear some of the students at the back of the classroom making fun of his Madeiran accent. The dialect is very different from the Portuguese spoken in the capital, almost a different language entirely. He sounds strange. He sounds poor. He sounds like an islander, and no one can really understand him. He loses his temper and threatens his teacher with a chair. He becomes the laughing stock of the class and he feels like an idiot. He is homesick for his family, his island and his friends. He calls home two or three times a week. It saddens him to hear his mother's voice; it makes him cry and miss her even more. Dolores tries to cheer him up, telling him to ignore the jokers at school. She often has to console him and convince him that his life and his future are over there in Lisbon, at the Sporting youth academy. In the end she has to fly out to the capital because Cristiano says he can't take it anymore. He wants to quit, abandon his dream and go home to the island so he can be with his family. It's a difficult first year, but gradually he adapts. Now, he concedes that he is grateful – to an extent – for the experience. 'In difficult times you learn a lot about yourself,' he has said. 'You have to stay strong and focus on what you really want.'

He needs that inner strength many years later to help him cope with the saddest day of his life. It is

Tuesday 6 September 2005. The following day Portugal will face Russia, a key moment in their quest to qualify for the 2006 World Cup. If they win and Slovakia concedes points, they will be one step closer to Germany. It is 9.00pm in Moscow. Cristiano is in his room watching a film when Portuguese manager Luiz Felipe Scolari summons him to his room. Portuguese captain Luís Figo is in the manager's hotel suite. Cristiano thinks it's a little odd to be meeting like this, but he suspects nothing. He presumes it must be about some strategic issue, something the coach and the captain want to discuss with him. But they have called him in to inform him of the death of his father. Dinis Aveiro has passed away at a clinic in London after being hospitalised several months earlier. His untimely death has been caused by alcohol and Cristiano is devastated. But despite his sadness he doesn't want to miss the match. 'I wanted to play. That was all I knew how to do,' he says later. 'I wanted to show everyone that I was able to compartmentalise, that I was a consummate professional and that I took my work seriously. I wanted to play that match in honour of my father. I wanted to score a goal for him. I was testing myself and all the people who love me.'

But the game against Russia ends in a 0–0 draw and he doesn't manage to score the goal that he wanted to dedicate to his father. He will do it at the World Cup in Germany instead, converting the final penalty against

England to take Portugal through to the semi-finals. He will raise his hand to the sky and say, 'This is for you, Dad.'

He returns home from Moscow to Madeira for the burial. He is dressed in a black shirt and sunglasses. With his family close to him at all times he manages to maintain his composure. He does not shed any tears, but his eyes suggest that he has done plenty of crying. Some time later, he will speak out regarding the way the press handled the death of his father, which was front-page news for the following four days. 'It really hurt me and my family. We needed peace and quiet, and it ended up becoming quite a commotion.'

In later years he pays tribute to Dinis: 'My father always encouraged me. He always told me to be ambitious and he was proud of my footballing achievements. I love him and I will always love him. He will always be with me. He will always be a role model to me. I like to think that wherever you are you will see what I am doing and what I have achieved.' Dinis disliked the cameras and the spotlight. He preferred to stay in the background but his relationship with his son was always strong. Before Cristiano went over to Lisbon, the two of them were inseparable. They remained close even when he moved to Manchester. Dinis was often with him, visiting him, supporting him and encouraging him until his illness would no longer allow it. Time and time again Cristiano tried to convince his father to check in to a clinic to treat his alcoholism, but he was unable to save him. Dinis continued drinking and there was nothing even England's best hospitals could do for him.

Without a doubt, his father's death is the toughest moment in his personal life. Meanwhile, on the pitch, the final of Euro 2004 on Sunday 4 July is probably one of the lowest points of his career. Portugal are the hosts and they are up against Greece at the Estádio de la Luz in Lisbon. For the first time in the history of the tournament, the two teams who played the inaugural match also meet in the final. On 13 June luck had been on Greece's side, as they beat the hosts 2–1 – a bitter, unexpected defeat, but one in which CR7 scored his first goal in a competitive match with his country. Just 23 days later, history is repeated, and the whole of Portugal watches, paralysed, for 90 minutes, unable to believe what is happening on the pitch. It doesn't matter that Portugal is one of the favourites for the title, nor that the bookies had a Greece win down at 80–1. And even the fact that Portugal haven't lost at either of Lisbon's Alvalade or Luz stadia in seventeen years cannot save them, nor the fact that they are the hosts – a decisive factor for Spain in 1964, Italy in 1968 and France in 1984. None of it matters.

The match ends 1–0 thanks to a header from Angelos Charisteas in the 57th minute. At the final whistle Ronaldo is in tears. Looking lost and alone in the centre of the pitch, he is oblivious to the consolatory words and gestures from his teammates, crying at the sadness of it all. And crying over missed chances, like in the 59th minute, when Nikopolidis thwarted him, or in the 74th, when he had acres of space in front of goal but he sent his shot over the bar, the 'ahhh!' from the crowd audible on the pitch. He is crying because he could never have imagined losing to Greece. Because 'we had a fantastic team and we have played a great tournament and we don't deserve to lose like this'. Because he's 'an ambitious person' and he wants to be 'the champion of Europe at nineteen years old'. 'But now I have to move on,' reflects Cristiano. 'I have to look forward. There will be many other opportunities to win in Europe throughout my career, and make up for this huge disappointment.'

It's not the only time the Portuguese will face tough times throughout the length of his career. The 2015–16 season proves to be one of the most challenging – even more so than during Mourinho's tenure. The season gets under way with Rafa Benítez taking the reins from Carlo Ancelotti. The new coach is a true 'Madridista' at heart, having started both his playing and coaching careers in the youth leagues with Real. Now he's back, having won La Liga twice with Valencia, the Champions League, the FA Cup and the Community Shield with Liverpool, the UEFA Europa League with Chelsea, the Italian Super Cup and Club World Cup with Inter Milan, and the Coppa Italia with Napoli. His credentials certainly speak for themselves. But it quickly becomes evident that something isn't quite right. Benítez and his players are not seeing eye to eye. There is speculation that he is trying to keep them on a short leash, implementing a level of discipline that will ensure he maintains complete control. But it's mission impossible when dealing with a roster of such huge stars with sky-high salaries, used to doing more or less whatever they please. Sparks fly almost immediately, particularly with CR7, with whom he has more than one run-in during training.

Following his arrival in the dugout, Benítez is asked time and again what he thinks of the Portuguese, and he always seems to beat about the bush in response. The first time is during pre-season in Australia: 'I had the misfortune of coming up against him in England when I was at Liverpool – he was a such a decisive force. He's a lot more mature now, well rounded and experienced. I think suffice to say he is one of the best players in the world.' When asked again a few weeks later, he is a little more effusive, but still restrained: 'I think he is an excellent player, one of the best I have coached. I can't say he's the best because I have been fortunate enough to work with many good players. But in terms of right now, he's our player and he's the best in the world.'

'Why can't you admit that Cristiano is the best?' a journalist probes on 16 September after a match against Shakhtar Donetsk. 'I'm surprised that you're all so interested in what one person thinks rather than what happens on the pitch,' replies Benítez, making no attempt to hide his desire to put an end to that particular line of questioning. 'Cristiano is the best in the world, I'm aware of his abilities, he demonstrates them in every match and every training session. He's the best in the world. From now on I'll say yes when you all ask, and then we can go back to focusing on what he actually does on the pitch.' But he is only playing to the gallery. Both the press and the fans are convinced that this is Real Madrid's annus horribilis, and they even suspect that the players are not giving it their all, in some form of boycott against the new coach. For the first time since his arrival at Real, there are an increasing number of voices calling for him to be sold to another club – for the right price, of course.

Things begin to spiral after the Christmas break, and Benítez is replaced by Zinedine Zidane. Cristiano doesn't hide his satisfaction when the dismissal goes public. 'We have lost a lot of time over this, he tells digital newspaper *El Confidencial.* Judging by a TV interview after La Liga is over – and following Benítez's departure to Newcastle – one of the biggest causes of tension between them appears to have been his insistence on teaching CR7 how to take free kicks. Letting out a loud, albeit somewhat forced, chuckle, Cristiano says: 'There are some things you can't even discuss with someone who has such a different opinion to your own. You just have to thank them and carry on. There is something to be learned from every coach, but there are also some things that can't be taught – you either have it or you don't. He worked with me on free kicks, but also the exact way to strike the ball and how to dribble.' Advice that did not seem to go down too well with Ronaldo, making it a chapter the footballer would probably rather forget.

With Benítez out of the picture, Ronaldo still faces plenty of challenges both on and off the pitch in the 2016–17 season. By the winter, despite having scored a similar number of goals to previous seasons, the crowd at the Bernabéu are starting to whistle at him during matches. 'Everyone in the world has someone who hates them, not just me,' he tells Chinese football publication *Dongqiudi* in January. After losing to Celta in the Copa del Rey, the whistles have become something of a statement among the Whites fans. 'I don't care about my critics, I'm here to satisfy my fans, who show me respect,' he concludes, before thanking the Chinese fans for voting him the *Dongqiudi* Most Valuable Player of 2016.

The whistling continues in subsequent matches, but it is not the only thorn in his side this season. In mid-June Madrid's regional state prosecutor formally accuses him of defrauding Spain's tax office between 2011 and 2014. It is alleged that he concealed income

from the sale of image rights through a financial structure that diverted the money via Ireland to a tax haven
in the British Virgin Islands, 'in order to conceal his
total income'. The figures cited are significant, and it is
estimated that he may have to pay a further €14.7 million in tax. Like Leo Messi he could also face the pros-
pect of a jail sentence, so Ronaldo, his lawyers and his
agent Jorge Mendes prepare themselves in the event of
a battle with the courts in the coming months.

Chapter 12

Followers

There is one arena in which Ronaldo is undoubtedly the reigning champion: social media. Online, he is unmatched. He has around 122 million likes on Facebook, having overtaken the singer Shakira in March 2015, who was the previous leader with 101 million. Following close behind, Real Madrid itself is now in second place, having overtaken Shakira in 2017. CR7 has 107 million followers on Instagram – more than Neymar Jr. He is the most popular athlete on Twitter, with more than 55 million followers, and he is eleventh overall, behind global celebrities such as Katy Perry, Justin Bieber and Taylor Swift.

And his popularity doesn't end there. According to data platform Hookit, on 23 February 2016 he becomes the first athlete to rack up a total of 200 million followers across Facebook, Twitter and Instagram – he is gaining 135,000 fans every day. He expresses his gratitude on Twitter. 'Really proud to be the first athlete with 200 million social media followers. A big thank you to all my fans!' he tweets, accompanied by a slew of happy and grateful emoticons.

One place and 78 million followers behind is Leo Messi – a considerable feat, since the Argentine still has no Twitter account. NBA basketball star LeBron James is in third place.

Cristiano joined Twitter in 2010, and has since posted around 2,900 tweets, around 40 a month, mostly in English. He follows fewer than 100 people, limiting it to world-famous celebrities such as Jennifer Lopez, Lady Gaga and Rafael Nadal, as well as footballers such as Sergio Ramos and his good friend Fábio Coentrão.

CR7's online appeal prompted him to launch his own community in 2013: vivaronaldo.com, a free site and app in English, where his fans could interact and keep up with the latest news on their idol. Users could follow all Cristiano's matches and enter competitions to win signed shirts or tickets to watch him play. They could also view exclusive photos and videos of events, connect with other fans, and interact with the player himself. The site wound down its activities in autumn 2015 – but not due to lack of success. In fact, the management company behind the venture promises exciting things in the pipeline. 'It's been a thrilling experience to power up such an amazing community of Cristiano fans for the last two and a half years. You can all keep supporting Cristiano on Viva Ronaldo's Facebook, Twitter and Instagram accounts.

Thank you all for being the Best Fans in the World! Stay tuned for the incredible products we're already developing. They will allow you to live and share your passions like never before!' reads the message on the homepage.

The key to garnering such a following has been CR7's willingness to share numerous moments in his life, both professional and personal. It fits with his open personality as much as with his business strategy. It is perhaps for that reason that the more reserved and fiercely private Messi is no match for his eternal rival when it comes to the online contest. There is an official 'Team Messi' Twitter account created and managed by his main sponsor that has more than 2 million followers, but currently no personal account. In fact, his family have often had to post statements to dispel rumours started by other Twitter users. As his sister has tweeted in the past: 'A message from Leo! Once again I would like to clarify that I do not have a Twitter account and I don't intend to create one for now. If I did, I would announce it via my Facebook page. I hope this clarifies things so that people don't get misled by any accounts that contain my name.'

But there is another Messi on Twitter: Matías Messi, Leo's brother. His tweets have caused quite a stir among football fans – for example, by asking why Real fans follow him if they dislike him so much. And although he clarified that he wasn't talking about all

Whites fans, the debate was already under way. He also caused a commotion when he posted a graphic comparing Leo and Cristiano's various titles dating back to 2009. All in support of Leo and his family, he insisted.

Social networks are clearly just another battleground for the world's biggest sports stars, or at least for their fans. It's a global contest that shows no sign of abating. It begins to build up just before a match or before an award such as the Ballon d'Or, and it gets particularly intense around a derby, when players are the subject of a torrent of insults alongside undying support. There are declarations of eternal love and hatred, commentary, analysis, articles, campaigns for and against. The web is a free-for-all where everyone has an opinion, and football – which leads the way in online sports chatter – sparks passionate debate. And although it's a team sport, it is the individual stars who command a lot of the attention online. Cristiano has far more Facebook followers than the official Real Madrid page (more than 105 million).

In that sense, Messi is unusual, in that he has 'only' 89 million followers, significantly fewer than Barcelona (102 million) as well as Cristiano. Although it's not his style to have such a public persona, the Flea has resigned himself to being present on the biggest social network, presumably conscious of the fact that when it comes to the business side of the footballing world, it's an extremely valuable promotional tool. Like CR7, he posts photos with his family, his teammates, or in the dressing room, as well as announcements from his sponsors. Both players are also present on Instagram and YouTube, and here again the Portuguese is also in the lead.

But despite being less active, Leo does benefit from the help of his club to amplify his reach. For example, to mark his 28th birthday on 24 June 2015, Barcelona challenges fans to flood the internet with photos, drawings, memes or any other original post to celebrate with the player, incorporating the hashtag #Messi28. It is the club's attempt to turn the date into a global event, and judging by the results, it's a success. Fans share videos of his best goals, pictures of him when he was little, or snaps of him with his trophies, as well as stats. An international tribute in every conceivable language.

In a report, Spanish newspaper *El Mundo* claimed that Messi and Ronaldo are part of a sizeable group of celebrities that have placed the management of their social media channels in the hands of professionals, and that their profiles are the result of intricately crafted communication strategies. Nothing is improvised, nothing is left to chance. This would explain Cristiano's meteoric rise on Facebook and Twitter, particularly since his third Ballon d'Or win. It has not gone unnoticed that the publicity juggernaut that surrounds him has stepped things up a notch since the beginning of 2015. He is now posting a lot more news items and seems almost omnipresent …

The press speculate that it's an attempt to counteract a dip in popularity due to months of negative press surrounding his personal life and questionable new friendships. In 2015 he experiences two extremely unpleasant incidents sparked by others' social media indiscretions. The first occurs during his 30th birthday celebrations in February, hot on the heels of Real's humiliating defeat by Atlético Madrid. It's ironic that it is precisely because of social media that the whole world finds out about his party, when someone decides to leak some pictures of him and most of the squad singing karaoke on stage and having a good time – too much of a good time by the fans' reckoning. The indiscreet person in question is Colombian musician Kevin Roldan – friend of James Rodríguez – whose posts only add fuel to the fire: 'Thank you for hiring me as the headline performer at your 30th birthday. It's an honour that you enjoy my music. It's going to be a very special night, I hope you enjoy the show. We're going to tear it up in Madrid tonight,' writes the reggaeton star just before the party. And after the event he uploads video and photos showing the player wearing a huge carnival-style hat.

Twitter erupts with vitriol and the hashtag #LaFiestaDeLaDeshonra ('shameful party'), which becomes a trending topic for the whole of the following day. The club can't explain why Cristiano – usually so fiercely private – hadn't taken more steps to keep the details of his ill-timed party under wraps. Even Casillas, Sergio Ramos and Ancelotti stayed away, perhaps conscious of how the whole spectacle could look. Jorge Mendes immediately tries to rectify the situation in a radio interview, saying that the footballer was 'distraught over the defeat' and that everyone at the party was trying to cheer him up. He also insists that the party had been planned more than a month in advance, that it couldn't have been cancelled, and that the star 'didn't want to be rude to those who had come'. Finally, he claims that the CR7 is considering suing Kevin Roldan, the only person who seems to have benefited from the scandal. 'There is no such thing as bad publicity,' declares the musician. 'The controversy has brought me new followers, downloads and visits to my site. Everything is a blessing from God.'

Towards the end of the year, the press are also pouncing on his frequent trips to Marrakech, particularly after he posts pictures online in the company of Moroccan professional kickboxer and martial artist Badr Hari. So far, nothing to write home about. But as always there are those who insist on pushing the issue, analysing every detail: the two men pictured arm in arm … in one shot Hari is carrying the player with the jokey caption 'Just Married' … in another they are surrounded by an all-male group of friends. In the pool, sunbathing, having dinner, and on a second hand private jet that the footballer bought for 19 million euros for these short getaways. And the ones who aren't interested in sentimental allusions instead focus on pointing out that Hari could be a bad influence on someone who has such a squeaky clean lifestyle. The 31-year-old Moroccan – whose ex-partner is the niece of football legend and former Barça coach Johan Cruyff – is known for violent outbursts which have earned him the nickname 'Badr Boy' – in a play on his first name. Born in Amsterdam, his police record includes a charge of attempted manslaughter, various assaults and a two-year prison sentence in 2012 for the aggravated assault of Dutch millionaire Koen Everink at a party.

Cristiano's public image has undoubtedly taken a hit, but he and his publicists manage to rectify it – with the help of social media. The key to their success is sharing moments of his life beyond the matches, training sessions and other public appearances. Within minutes the photos, opinions and messages are seen, read, commented on and reposted by millions of followers around the world, enabling them to close the gap between the player and mere mortals. He tweets to say how he is or that Real are going to win, or he shares his holiday snaps. Sometimes he works all his followers up into a frenzy over a single photo, like the one he uploaded at the end of July 2015 captioned 'stretching time'. It was just a snap taken during a session with one of the Real Madrid physios, but the sight of his muscles coupled with a distinct lack of clothing caused quite a stir.

The sporting elite have found a way to boost their personal profiles and brands in a global, immediate and cost-effective way. Fans feel that their idols are talking directly to them, and they can respond. In reality, it's part of a well-oiled publicity machine that tells the stories of the players' lives and reinforces their brand every day thanks to the power of the web.

Chapter 13

Money

A football-shaped meteor has fallen somewhere on Earth. Ronaldo receives a call: 'The boots have arrived.' He leaps into them and he is transformed. He is a superhero capable of galactic speeds. He can leap from building to building like Spider-man. He has the city at his feet. After a few circuits around the globe he lands on the pitch at the Bernabéu. And all thanks to Nike. The global sports giant has spared no expense in riding the media tidal wave in the lead-up to one of the most hyped matches in football: the Real Madrid–Barça *Clásico*. CR7 is a big asset for the company – they know that almost everything he touches turns to gold. The 'brand Ronaldo' attributes are competitiveness and hard work, professionalism and sacrifice, a desire to win and irreverence. He is particularly compatible with the Nike brand.

In addition, the Real star is a natural performer, extremely comfortable in front of the camera. He does not bat an eyelid at being made up, posing for long photo shoots, and repeating the same movements over and over for the camera. He enjoys playing the starring role. A set, for him, is just an extension of the football pitch, where he is always number one. It's just another form of performance, albeit a little different from what he does every weekend. And because of that, he approaches promoting trainers with the same determination as he would making a run at goal.

In fact, Ronaldo's commitment to his sponsors often seems to go above and beyond his contractual obligations. In a training session at the beginning of 2014, his then teammate Xabi Alonso challenged him over whether Adidas or Nike made the best boots, criticising the fact that he wore 'plastic' trainers made by a 'basketball brand'. Ronaldo froze in astonishment at what he was hearing, before waving his arms wildly, insisting that these were the shoes of a star player. It was a small private disagreement that happened to be captured by a TV camera, but it could almost have been a scripted advert. Funnily enough, at the time he was also wearing a sweatshirt made by Adidas, who sponsor Real Madrid.

On an individual level, while Nike is team Cristiano, Adidas is team Messi. Even in sponsorship deals they are rivals. After a long legal battle, the German sports brand won Messi from Nike, who had sponsored him since he was fourteen years old. He signed an extremely lucrative contract with Adidas in 2006, just before the Germany World Cup. So, what does Leo Messi sell? 'Authenticity,' claims Fernando Solanas, former head of sport marketing at Adidas Iberia. Fair enough, but what is his appeal off the pitch? 'He is just, quite simply, himself, a guy who loves being with his family, his friends, his people. Too often sportsmen seem to live in a distant universe, very far removed from our world. Leo, with his shyness, is close to all football fans.' But it's more than that. From early on in his professional career, the image of Messi was that of a boy who succeeded in reaching the top despite his height and growth problems. In that sense, he symbolises Adidas's 2007 campaign slogan 'Impossible is nothing'. With hard work, perseverance and strong will, he has demonstrated and continues to demonstrate to the wider world that nothing is impossible.

Messi does not have the same self-assuredness and ease in front of the camera, nor the same physique or demeanour as Ronaldo. But he has still made some bold choices. He has been a face of Dolce & Gabbana for many years, modelling underwear as well as sporting the Italian designers' famously eye-catching suits at various Ballon d'Or galas. Now, however, he prefers Armani … a brand for which CR7 has also modelled underwear. Leo still has plenty of muscles to show off – although the Portuguese is rather more fond of showing his, and has even launched his own brand, CR7 Underwear. His foray into modelling began with a campaign for Armani in 2010–11, taking inspiration from former Man United star David Beckham, who modelled for the brand together with wife Victoria from 2007. Cristiano is depicted as the epitome of the masculine sex symbol, fulfilling the Greek ideal of beauty and health. The advert has become the second most viewed fashion video on YouTube, topped only by the world premiere of Lady Gaga's Bad Romance, played at Alexander McQueen's Spring/Summer 2010 catwalk show, the designer's final collection before his death.

Not to be left behind, Messi's promos for Turkish Airlines have been a resounding success. In the first two, he appears with LA Lakers star and die-hard Barça fan Kobe Bryant, who has expressed a desire to finish his basketball career with the Barcelona team. In the 2012 advert, they try to better each other's tricks with the ball while on board a plane to see who can impress a little boy who is a fellow passenger, garnering more than 112 million views on YouTube. They follow it up in 2013 with a Kobe vs Messi 'selfie shootout', where the two compete to see who can take the most pictures of themselves in different locations, and which Bryant eventually wins by photo-bombing his rival in Istanbul. It has had more than 144 million views and has been voted the best ad of the decade on YouTube. In 2014 the airline would replace Bryant with Didier Drogba, and show the former Chelsea star flying around the world trying to find ever more remote and exotic restaurants to eat at, always spotting a photo on the wall that reveals Messi got there first. Yet another funny ad that has racked up more than 62 million views.

Back to the rivalry in question, it is clear that Leo and Cristiano can sell pretty much anything, in any corner of the world. Their faces are instantly recognisable. 'They are global enterprises in a market where agents find them the most lucrative opportunities,' opines Patrick Mignon, sociologist at the National Institute of Sport and Physical Education in Paris. 'A top player is like a Louis Vuitton bag or a Cartier ring,' adds Gunter Gebauer, professor of philosophy at the Institute for Sports Science at the University of Hanover. 'They are a marketable brand of their own.'

And there is no better example of that than the fact that Ronaldo has decided to sell 50 per cent of all his image rights to Singaporean tycoon Peter Lim, the largest shareholder of Primera División club Valencia, who is also a personal friend of Ronaldo's agent Jorge Mendes. CR7 announces the deal on his Facebook page: 'I am very excited to announce my latest deal with Mint Media, owned by my good friend, businessman Peter Lim from Singapore, to acquire my image rights. This is a very strategic move for me and my management team to take the Cristiano Ronaldo brand to the next level, especially in Asia.' The owner of the other 50 per cent of his image rights is, of course, Real Madrid, which also has a special interest in the Asian market and has already organised several summer tours around the continent. The more global fans, the more the club can make in rights and marketing.

There is no doubt that Messi and Ronaldo have cross-border and mass audience appeal as advertising icons and brand ambassadors. Dozens of companies feature them in adverts, publicity material and campaigns to raise awareness and break into new markets.

They promote trainers, airlines, underwear, shavers, videogames consoles, drinks, banks, jeans, sportswear, cars, aftershave, sweets, toys, phones, TVs, watches, comics, shampoo, instant messaging services … Countless brands have taken a gamble on them, and continue to do so. Ronaldo promotes Nike, Altice, Abott, Herbalife, TAG Heuer, PokerStars, Sacoor Brothers, Clear, XTrade, Monster, Sixpad Training Gear … while Messi promotes Adidas, Pepsi, Gatorade, Lays, FIFA 16, Gillette, Ooredoo, EA Sports, Tata Motors, Space Scooter, Armani, Huawei … This list is endless. Occasionally they are contracted by the same brand, as is the case with Samsung. The electronics brand has produced some memorable adverts, including one where Messi turns into Marvel Comics' Iron Man as part of the mobile division's promotion of the upcoming *Avengers* movie. And there's even one which features both players as part of 'Galaxy XI', the team that will 'save the world'. 'We have created a dream team with some of the best players in the world, who have united as Galaxy XI to bring this story to life through various channels and

Samsung Galaxy devices,' explains Younghee Lee, Samsung's executive vice-president of global marketing, when the advert is first aired. Messi and Ronaldo are joined by Germany's Mario Götze, Brazil's Oscar dos Santos, China's Wu Lei, Italy's Stephan El Shaarawy, Nigeria's Victor Moses, Colombia's Radamel Falcao, South Korea's Lee Chung-Yong, Spain's Íker Casillas, England's Wayne Rooney, the United States' Landon Donovan and Russia's Aleksandr Kerzhakov. Their coach is Germany's Franz Beckenbauer.

Messi and Ronaldo star in plenty of apocalyptic adverts, or ones in which they are superheroes. But they have also made some more risky decisions over their image. Cristiano, for example, starred in an advert for the Facial Fitness Pao, an unusual facial exercise product intended to tone facial muscles. But all these decisions are weighed very carefully, as there are millions of pounds at stake for both sides. Nike, for example, who made Cristiano the face of their Brazil 2014 World Cup campaign, calculated that Portugal's failure to qualify – or, in other words, the absence of CR7 from the World Cup finals – would have a negative impact on the brand equating to the loss of €10 million.

Another thing to consider is that their value fluctuates as much as the stock market. Winning a prize such as the Ballon d'Or could tip the balance. Which is why the list of highest-earning footballers can shift back and forth. Of course, when it comes to income it's not just about publicity campaigns. *Forbes* magazine has the Portuguese in the lead, at least for the moment, earning 58 million dollars a year in salary and bonuses. On top of that there's a nice bit of sponsorship cash which amounted to 35 million dollars in 2016, making a dizzying 93 million dollars a year. CR7 is not only the highest paid footballer on the planet for the third year running, he is now the top earner across all team sports worldwide.

If the figures are correct – although it's difficult to verify in the opaque world of football – Leo Messi is in second place. The Argentine earns 53 million dollars in salary and bonuses, plus 27 million in sponsorship deals. He brings in around 13 million a year less than CR7, but they both significantly outstrip Neymar, who is in third place with 37 million dollars in 2016.

They are record breakers in every aspect of their careers. Every contract negotiation becomes a dance over figures that would make mere mortals dizzy. CR7's move from Man United to Real Madrid in 2009 breaks the transfer record at the time thanks to a fee of €94 million (£80 million). The figure provokes a wave of reaction and comment – some think it's a positive investment, while others cannot fathom such a dispro-portionate amount.

And in recent years, Cristiano has taken care to renegotiate his terms with Real. In November 2016 he renewed his contract with club president Florentino

Pérez until 2021, putting him on €18 million a season, still €2 million less than the unofficial figure Barça pays Messi, which according to the press is around €20 million. But CR7 insists that 'there are things in life more important than money. Yes, it is important, but it's not the top priority.' The Flea would surely agree with that sentiment, despite the fact that every time these two stars sign new contracts, the numbers seem to contain more and more zeros.

They are goal-scoring and money-making machines – and they try to outdo each other in both arenas. They might be the most expensive players, but they are also the most profitable. *Forbes* can vouch for that. According to the magazine, although the two stars earn infinitely more than everyone else, one has to take into account that they score so many goals and create even more. And that can only serve to line the coffers of their respective clubs, which, incidentally, are the two most valuable in the world. In short, it's worth paying the price for them. It's about more than just football. As former Real and Argentina player Jorge Valdano notes, it's about entertainment, showbusiness, creating a stunning spectacle. And it's impossible to put a price on dreams – at least for now.

Career records

Lionel Andrés Messi

Nicknames: Leo, La Pulga ('the Flea')
Born: Rosario, Santa Fe, Argentina, 24 June 1987
Nationality: Argentine
Parents: Jorge and Celia
Brothers: Matías and Rodrigo
Sister: María Sol
Wife: Antonella Roccuzzo
Sons: Thiago, Mateo
Position: Striker
Shirt number: 10
Height: 169 cm
Weight: 67 kg

Clubs
Grandoli (1992–1994)
Club Atlético Newell's Old Boys (1994–2001)
FC Barcelona (2001–present)

Barcelona

First team debut: 16 November 2003
against FC Porto (away)
La Liga debut: 16 October 2004
against RCD Espanyol (away)
First goal: 1 May 2005 against Albacete (home)

Appearances (up to 22 July 2017)
La Liga 382 – Goals 349
Cups 77 – Goals 56
Europe 119 – Goals 97
Total matches played 583 – Goals 507

Argentina

Debut: 17 August 2005 vs Hungary (away)
First goal: 1 March 2006 vs Croatia (away)
Caps 141 – Goals 74 (up to 9 June 2017)

Tournaments
Under-20 World Cup 2005
World Cup 2006, 2010, 2014
Copa América 2007, 2011, 2015, 2016
Summer Olympics 2008

Team honours

Barcelona
La Liga: 8 (2004–05, 2005–06, 2008–09, 2009–10,
2010–11, 2012–13, 2014–15, 2015–16)

Copa del Rey: 5 (2008–09, 2011–12, 2014–15,
2015–16, 2016–17)
Spanish Super Cup: 7 (2005, 2006, 2009, 2010,
2011, 2013, 2016)
UEFA Champions League: 4 (2005–06, 2008–09,
2010–11, 2014–15)
UEFA Super Cup: 3 (2009, 2011, 2015)
FIFA Club World Cup: 3 (2009, 2011, 2015)

Argentina
Under-20 World Cup 2005
Olympic gold medal, Beijing 2008

Individual honours
Golden Ball (player of the tournament),
FIFA World Cup 2014
FIFA Ballon d'Or 2010, 2011, 2012, 2015
European Golden Shoe 2010, 2012, 2013, 2017
Ballon d'Or 2009
FIFA World Player of the Year 2009
Onze d'Or 2009
Alfredo Di Stéfano trophy 2008–09
UEFA Champions League Top Scorer 2008–09
UEFA Club Forward of the Year 2008–09
UEFA Club Footballer of the Year 2008–09
LFP Best Player 2008–09
European Player of the Year (second place) 2008
FIFA World Player of the Year (second place) 2007, 2008

FIFA The Best (second place) 2016

Ballon d'Or (second place) 2016

Under-21 European Footballer of the Year 2007

European Player of the Year (third place) 2007

European FIFA Under-20 World Cup Top Scorer 2005

FIFA Under-20 World Cup Player of the Tournament 2005

Copa América Young Player of the Tournament 2007

Player of the Year, Argentina 2005, 2007

FIFPro Special Young Player of the Year 2006–07, 2007–08

FIFPro World Young Player of the Year 2005–06,
2006–07, 2007–08

World Soccer Young Player of the Year 2005–06,
2006–07, 2007–08

Premio Don Balón (Best Foreign Player in La Liga)
2006–07, 2008–09

EFE Trophy (Best Ibero-American Player in La Liga)
2006–07, 2008–09

FIFPro World XI 2006–07, 2007–08, 2008–09

Cristiano Ronaldo dos Santos Aveiro

Nicknames: CR7, CR9, Cris

Born: Funchal, Madeira, Portugal – 5 February 1985

Nationality: Portuguese

Parents: José Dinis (died 6 September 2005)

and María Dolores

Sisters: Katia and Elma

Brother: Hugo

Son: Cristiano Junior

Position: Winger

Shirt number: 7

Height: 186 cm

Weight: 85 kg

Clubs

Andorinha (1993–1995)

Nacional (1995–1997)

Sporting Lisbon (1997–2003)

Manchester United (2003–2009)

Real Madrid (2009–present)

Sporting Lisbon

First team debut: 14 July 2002, friendly

against Olympique Lyonnais

League debut: 7 October 2002 against Moreirense FC

First goal: 3 August 2002, friendly against Real Betis

Appearances

League 25 – Goals 3

Cups 3 – Goals 2

Europe 3 – Goals 0

Manchester United

Debut: 16 August 2003, Premier League match against
Bolton Wanderers

First goal: 1 November 2003 against Portsmouth

Appearances

Premier League 196 – Goals 86

Cups 38 – Goals 17

Europe 55 – Goals 16

Real Madrid

Debut: 21 July 2009, friendly against Shamrock Rovers

La Liga debut: 29 August 2009

against Deportivo de La Coruña

First goal: 29 July 2003, friendly

against Liga Deportiva Universitaria de Quito

Appearances (up to 24 July 2017)

La Liga 265 – Goals 285

Cups 36 – Goals 25

Europe 89 – Goals 92

Portugal

Debut: 20 August 2003, friendly against Kazakhstan

First goal: 12 June 2004 against Greece in the opening
match of UEFA Euro 2004

Caps 143 – Goals 75 (up to 28 June 2017)

Tournaments

UEFA Euro 2004, 2008, 2012, 2016

FIFA World Cup 2006, 2010, 2014

Team honours

Manchester United

UEFA Champions League: 1 (2008)

Premier League: 3 (2007, 2008, 2009)

FA Cup: 1 (2004)

League Cup: 2 (2006, 2009)

FIFA Club World Cup: 1 (2008)

Community Shield: 2 (2007, 2008)

Real Madrid

La Liga: 2011–12, 2016–17

Copa del Rey: 2011, 2014

Spanish Super Cup: 2012

UEFA Champions League: 2013–14, 2015–16, 2016–17

UEFA Super Cup: 2014, 2016

FIFA Club World Cup: 2014, 2016

Portugal
UEFA Euro 2016

Individual honours
Ballon d'Or 2008, 2016
FIFA Ballon d'Or 2013, 2014
FIFA World Player of the Year 2008
FIFA The Best 2016
European Golden Shoe 2008, 2011, 2014, 2015
PFA Players' Player of the Year 2007, 2008
PFA Young Player of the Year 2007
Sir Matt Busby Player of the Year 2004, 2007, 2008
UEFA Champions League Top Scorer 2016–17

Acknowledgements

I would like to thank Duncan Heath, Philip Cotterell, Robert Sharman, Michael Sells, Sheli Rodney, Estela Celada, Laure Merle d'Aubigné and Roberto Domínguez.

Dedicated to Olmo, Lorenzo, Elvira, Alda and Tullio.